Accounting for the Cost of Interest

Accounting for the Cost of Interest

Robert N. Anthony
Harvard University

Lexington Books
D.C. Heath and Company
Lexington, Massachusetts
Toronto   London

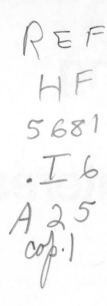

Library of Congress Cataloging in Publication Data

Anthony, Robert Newton, 1916
    Accounting for the cost of interest.

    Includes bibliographical references and index.
    1. Interest and usury. 2. Accounting. I. Title.
HF5681.I6A25   657'.74   75-12484
ISBN 0-669-00027-2

Published simultaneously in Canada

Printed in the United States of America

International Standard Book Number: 0-669-00027-2

Library of Congress Catalog Card Number: 75-12484

Contents

List of Tables and Figures

Table

Figure

Preface

The proposal advanced in this book stems from frustrations that I have experienced over the past fifteen years in attempting to deal with certain practical business problems. These problems involved the question of interest in a variety of contexts, and the frustrations are related to the fact that the treatment of interest in accounting is fundamentally different from the economic reality of interest.

In the 1950s, while working on problems involving lease financing, I was bothered by the fact that the cost of using a leased asset included interest, whereas the cost of using an equivalent purchased asset did not. In attempting to develop a rational approach to measuring the performance of profit-center managers, it was frustrating to find that the then newly developed present-value techniques for measuring the profitability of a proposed investment could not be reconciled with the conventional method of accounting for the profitability of that investment after it had been made. A capital acquisition could actually cause a decrease in the profits reported for the early years after the asset became productive, even though the profit center was in fact more profitable.

As assistant secretary of defense, in discussing the question of allowable costs on defense contracts, I ran up against the argument that the interest cost of debt capital was a cost because accounting said it was, whereas the interest cost of equity capital was not a cost because accounting said it was not. This argument, if accepted, would have resulted in irrational policies on the pricing of defense contracts. In developing the rules for justifying price increases in the Phase II price control program, I was frustrated by the fact that accounting data on product costs did not include an allowance for return on capital employed.

For a long time I accepted as inevitable the difference between the accounting and the economic treatment of interest. The possibility of an alternative treatment was either not mentioned in accounting texts and journal articles, or it was regarded as impractical; I concluded that solutions to problems such as those I faced had to be arrived at by departing from financial accounting principles. This was not a satisfying conclusion, because as an accountant, I believe strongly that discrepancies between financial accounting information and the information needed by decision-makers should be restricted to those necessary to meet the criterion of objectivity, which is of great importance in financial accounting. Eventually, I began to wonder whether the long-accepted treatment of interest in financial accounting really was inevitable. This led to the proposal described in this book.

In the course of working on the problem (which has occupied me off and on since 1967), I ran across a body of literature from the early twentieth century, including one excellent piece written on my own campus, in which the recognition in accounting of the interest cost of both debt and equity capital was seriously advocated. Thus, mine is not a new proposal. Nevertheless, for the past forty years, very little has been written on the subject, and there has been very little discussion of it. It may be appropriate, then, to call it a rejuvenated proposal. In any event, I hope readers will become sufficiently intrigued to pursue the subject further, and that their support will, before too long, lead to action by the Financial Accounting Standards Board.

Acknowledgments

An abridged version of this proposal has appeared in the *Harvard Business Review* (November-December 1973). I appreciate the encouragement of its editor, Ralph F. Lewis, and the suggestions of the associate editor, Walter C. McBeth, Jr.

In 1973, Professor Robert Sterling, Director of Research of the American Accounting Association, appointed a committee to advise me on this project: George C. Catlett, Arthur Andersen & Co.; Professors Nicholas Dopuch, University of Chicago; Kenneth S. Most, Texas A & M University; Melvin C. O'Connor, Michigan State University; Charles H. Smith, University of Texas at Austin; and Earl A. Spiller, Jr., Washington University. Their suggestions were of inestimable help in broadening, clarifying, and revising the ideas contained in an earlier draft. Charles Smith provided twenty-eight typewritten pages of thoughtful comments on both substance and arrangement. Earl Spiller gave many new insights into conceptual problems.

I also appreciate comments from: Professor Sidney Davidson, dean of the Graduate School of Business, University of Chicago; Professor R. Lee Brummet, School of Business Administration, University of North Carolina; Philip L. Defliese, Coopers & Lybrand; Paul Jeynes, former engineering economist, Public Service Electric & Gas Company; Professor Dan T. Smith, Graduate School of Business, Stanford University; Leonard Spacek, Arthur Andersen & Co.; Robert T. Sprouse, Financial Accounting Standards Board; Donald J. Trawicki, Touche, Ross & Co.; Bruce F. Young, Young and Associates; and Professors M. Edgar Barrett, J. Keith Butters, Gerald Johnson, A.C. Lyles, James S. Reece, John K. Shank, and Richard F. Vancil, colleagues at the Harvard Business School.

Research by Martha A. Dula and Alfred E. Kraft is also acknowledged with appreciation, as is the editorial assistance of Judith A. Auerbach, the suggestions of Max Hall, and the secretarial help of Ann T. Carter.

Financial support for the project was provided by the Division of Research, Harvard Business School, from funds provided by the Associates of the School.

The views expressed herein are my own and not necessarily those of the persons named above. In fact, some of them strongly disagree.

Accounting for the Cost of Interest

1

An Overview of the Proposal

In economics, the word *interest* refers to the cost of using capital. The definition of interest in financial accounting differs from its economics definition in two fundamental respects. First, in financial accounting, interest refers only to the charge for using *debt* capital; accountants do not record a charge for the use of *equity* capital. Second, in financial accounting, interest is not ordinarily treated as an element of cost in the sense that labor and material are so treated; rather, interest on debt capital is regarded as an expense that is deducted in full from the revenues of the period in which the interest is incurred.

This book argues that accounting should adopt the concept of interest used in economics. Specifically, it is proposed that interest on the use of both debt and equity capital should be accounted for as an item of cost—the cost of using capital—and that it should be recorded in the same way as other items of cost are recorded, namely:

The cost of goods manufactured should include an interest charge for the use of capital tied up in the plant and equipment involved in the manufacturing process, and inventory amounts should include this interest cost.

The cost of assets held for sale or use in future periods, such as petroleum reserves, should include the interest cost of holding these assets.

The cost of new plant assets should include interest on the capital used during the construction process. (Once an asset has been put into productive use, no further interest cost would be accumulated for it.)

The interest cost of an accounting period in excess of the amounts included in the asset items listed above should be charged as an expense of the period.

These rules correspond to the generally accepted accounting practices for other items of cost, such as labor; the labor used on products becomes a part of the cost of these products and is included in their inventory amounts; labor used to construct plant is a part of the cost of the plant, and the other labor cost of the period is reported as a period expense, as general and administrative expense.

This proposal is not new. In the early decades of the twentieth century a similar proposal was vigorously advocated and hotly debated. The debate subsided in the late 1920s, and although a few accounting theoreticians

1

have discussed the possibility in more recent years, the business community has given practically no thought to the possibility of changing generally accepted accounting principles so as to incorporate such a proposal.

This chapter summarizes the conceptual foundations for the proposal; its advantages in financial accounting, in public policy issues, and in management accounting; and the practical ways in which it can be implemented. Each of these topics is discussed in detail in later chapters.

Conceptual Foundations

Economics describes principles that govern the operation of a business, and financial accounting measures and reports the results of business operations. One would therefore expect that the principles of financial accounting would be consistent with the principles of economics, unless there were good reasons for a divergence. The burden of proof should be on those who seek to justify such a divergence.

Nevertheless, the inconsistency between the accounting and the economic treatment of interest is taken for granted by a great many people. When the possibility of recording interest as a cost is suggested, the invariable response is that such a practice would not be in accordance with generally accepted accounting principles. This book shows that two basic accounting concepts—the entity concept and the cost concept—*do* support the recording of interest as a cost.

In the nineteenth century, accounting was governed by what is called the *proprietary* concept: assets were considered as owned by the proprietors, and liabilities were considered as liabilities of the proprietors. With such a concept there was no point in attempting to record the cost of using equity capital separately from the profit earned by the business, since both the capital charge and the profit "belonged" to the proprietors. With the development of publicly owned corporations, the basic idea of accounting shifted from the proprietary concept to the *entity* concept; the corporation was viewed as an entity entirely separate from its proprietors. This entity obtained its capital from two principal sources; debt capital came from creditors, and equity capital came from shareholders. Equity capital, therefore, became just another source of funds. Under these circumstances, it would seem appropriate to measure the cost of using the equity capital which is supplied by outside investors, just as it is appropriate to measure the cost of using debt capital, which is also furnished by outside parties. From the standpoint of the entity, each type of capital is a resource furnished by an outside party. In this book, the term *interest* is used for the cost of using both types of capital—debt capital and equity capital.

The second basic accounting concept is the cost concept. Assets are initially recorded at their cost. Costs that expire in a given accounting period are called expenses. Net income is the difference between revenues and expenses. If interest is in fact a cost, it should be recorded as an element of the initial cost of assets that require the use of capital, and should attach to the asset amount until the asset becomes an expense. For example, manufactured goods should be recorded in inventory at amounts that include the interest cost of the capital employed in the manufacturing process, and this interest cost should be one element of expense in the period in which these goods are sold.

Cost measures the amount of resources used for some purpose. In manufacturing a product, a company uses a resource called labor, which is measured by salaries, wages, and related fringe benefits; it uses another resource called material, which is measured by material costs; and it uses resources that are collectively called services, which are measured by utility costs, rentals, and similar items. A business also uses capital; that is, it obtains funds which it uses to acquire assets. Those who have this capital, whether lenders or shareholders, will not furnish it to a company unless they anticipate receiving a reward for doing so. Capital therefore has a cost; it is called interest. Interest represents the cost of using someone else's capital, just as rent is a cost of using someone else's building.

Those who maintain that interest should be treated differently from labor, material, or services costs should be able to demonstrate that there is something about the nature of interest that makes it fundamentally different from these other elements of cost. In chapter 2, possible differences are examined, and the conclusion is drawn that they are not, in fact, fundamental.

Although interest on total capital is not recorded as a cost in financial accounting—that is, in the accounting that governs the preparation of financial statements prepared for the use of investors and other external parties—the concept that the use of capital does have a cost and that this cost should be explicitly recognized is well accepted in the internal accounting that serves as an aid to management.

For example, in analyzing a proposed capital acquisition, a relatively new but widely accepted approach is to include among the relevant costs not only the cost of the asset itself, but also the cost of the capital used to acquire the asset. In arriving at selling prices, many companies take into account the cost of the capital employed in making the product. In measuring the profitability of a division or other profit center, many companies use the residual income method, in which a capital charge is subtracted from profits computed in the conventional manner. The capital charge corresponds to interest as the term is used here.

The foregoing summary of the conceptual underpinnings of the proposal is brief, and I well recognize that it will not convince skeptics. I trust that they will be willing to suspend judgment until they have read the more thorough discussion of these points in chapter 2.

Implications of the Proposal

Recording interest as a cost would have a greater impact on the numbers reported in balance sheets and income statements than any change since the introduction of depreciation accounting. It also has implications for the use of accounting information in public policy discussions and in taxation, rate regulation, contract pricing, and other government activities. It will increase the harmonization of management accounting information with financial accounting information. Its implication in each of these areas is described briefly below, and discussed in detail in chapters 3, 4, and 5.

Implications for Financial Accounting

If the economic facts of interest were recorded in the accounts, readers of financial statements would have a clearer understanding of the status and performance of a business.

Except in public utilities, a building constructed by a company's own personnel appears on the books at a lower cost than an identical building constructed by an outside contractor, because no interest cost is counted for a self-constructed building. There is no logical reason for omitting interest costs for self-constructed buildings and including them for purchased buildings, nor for treating buildings built for public utilities differently than buildings built for other companies.

The longer an item remains in inventory, the greater is its real cost to the company. The amount of this additional cost is immaterial in companies where inventory turns over frequently, but it is of considerable importance in companies that hold inventories for significantly long periods of time. Accounting does not recognize this cost, and accounting therefore understates the cost of inventories held for long periods of time.

The return that a company earns on its equity capital consists of two elements, interest and profit. In current practice, these elements are combined in the single number labelled "net income." Although all the production and marketing activities of a company contribute to the generation of income, accounting recognizes the return only as of the time when the product is sold. In effect, therefore, accounting reports that all the return on capital is earned by the marketing organization, and none of it by the production organization. If interest were recorded as a cost that is incurred throughout the operating cycle, the offsetting credit would show that a return on capital was correspondingly being earned throughout the cycle.

If the interest component of return on capital were accounted for separately, the amount reported on the "bottom line" of the income statement would be smaller than it now is. Net income, on the proposed basis, would show how much a company earned over and above a minimum charge for the cost of the capital that it used. The amount would be a good measure of performance, for a company has not performed satisfactorily if it has not generated enough revenue to cover all its costs, including the cost of using capital. This net income amount would not be affected substantially by the relative amount of debt and equity in a company's capital structure; the debt/equity ratio has a great influence on the net income amount in current practice.

Additions to shareholders' equity during a period would come from two sources, the charge for equity interest and net income. The sum of these two amounts would differ somewhat from the present credit that corresponds to net income because of timing differences arising from the interest cost that is embedded in assets, but over a period of years the total of shareholders' equity would not be materially affected by the proposal.

Public Policy Implications

Many government agencies use accounting information they obtain from business firms. Including interest as an element of cost would facilitate the work of these agencies. The process of rate setting by regulatory agencies would be simpler and more straightforward. Price controls could be designed on the principle that prices should provide a fair return on capital employed. The Department of Defense and other government agencies, which now arrive at the price on cost-type contracts by using a profit margin that is essentially a percentage of estimated cost, could shift to the much more equitable basis that takes into account the amount of capital employed.

Although the proposal per se does not contemplate a change in the basis of calculating income for tax purposes, there are advantages in adopting a similar principle for income tax calculations. The fact that interest expense on debt is tax deductible, while no deduction is allowed for the corresponding cost of using equity capital, has some undesirable social consequences. These would be removed if a minimum interest cost on equity capital were allowed as a business expense.

It is difficult to convince people that a business must earn enough to cover the cost of its capital if it is to survive. This message would come through to the public more clearly if the cost of using capital were labeled for what it is—a real cost. Although a few people may claim that any amount of profit above the minimum cost of capital is unwarranted, the general public would undoubtedly regard the net income amount as a reward for good performance, which is essential in our economic system. In any event, the calculations that now "prove" that profits are a large fraction of the sales dollar, or of the GNP, could no longer be made. As a related point, the consumer wonders why profit margins, expressed as a percentage of sales, vary so widely among companies of various types. Since one important reason for these differences is the difference in the amount of capital employed, the facts would be clearer if interest were counted as an element of cost.

Harmonizing Financial Accounting and Management Accounting

Although no law or principle requires that the internal accounting information used in managing a business be consistent with the financial accounting reports prepared for outside parties, such consistency has at least two advantages. First, it reduces the need for two sets of books. Second, there is a widespread belief that financial accounting numbers are "real" numbers and that numbers constructed according to something other than financial accounting principles are "soft" or even "phony." Many people, probably the majority, do not believe that equity interest is a real cost, despite what the economics books say and despite the fact that, when they stop to think about it, they know full well that equity capital cannot be obtained without cost. If financial accounting recognized equity interest as a real cost, this misconception would be overcome. Consequently, there would be an increasing acceptance within a business of measurements of profit-center performance that incorporate a charge for capital employed and of the importance of recognizing interest costs in calculations of economic order quantity, in determining appropriate inventory levels, in optimizing working capital amounts, in pricing, and in other business decisions.

Implementation of the Proposal

A proposal to record interest on both debt and equity capital as a cost has no practical significance without a feasible way of implementing it. Two practical problems arise. The first, and by far the more important, is the problem of measuring the interest cost of equity capital. The second problem is the largely procedural one of deciding how interest cost should be incorporated in the accounts.

Measuring the Cost of Using Capital

A sharp distinction is often made between the problem of measuring the cost of debt capital and that of measuring the cost of equity capital; the former is regarded as easy to measure and the latter, as impossible. Neither characterization is accurate.

In measuring the interest cost of debt capital, difficulties arise in measuring the interest cost on bonds that are sold at a discount or at a premium; in adjusting for the call premium and unamortized discount when a bond issue is refunded; in measuring the cost of convertible bonds sold at a yield that is significantly less than the going rate of debt interest; and in imputing a cost to certain debt instruments in which the interest and principal components are deliberately not shown separately. In all these situations, pronouncements of the Accounting Principles Board require that an approximation of the true annual interest cost be reported in the income statement. The calculations required to arrive at this cost can be quite complicated. Nevertheless, the accounting profession tackles these problems, and it is increasingly willing to use complicated procedures in order to find the true interest cost of debt capital.

Admittedly, there is no precise way of measuring the interest rate applicable to equity capital. Although there is a vast literature on the subject, no one has yet described a method of making a precise measurement that is widely accepted as being valid, that is applicable to companies generally, and that is sufficiently objective to be used as a basis for financial reporting. Nor is anyone likely to do so. Businessmen do, nonetheless, make judgments that explicitly or implicitly involve such a rate. Alternatively, they use a number that approximates the average interest rate for both debt and equity; but since the rate for debt interest is calculable, the rate for equity interest can be deduced from this average.

Since the nineteenth century, the estimated cost of using capital has been an element in the calculation of rates for regulated public utilities. In analyses involving proposed capital investments, the majority of industrial companies use a required earnings rate, a required rate of return, or some comparable number. Companies that use the residual income method of measuring divisional performance must compute a "capital charge" as one element of a division's cost.

In devising a principle for measuring interest cost for financial reporting purposes, the approaches used for other purposes provide a good starting point, but some special considerations must be taken into account: (1) the method must be applicable to all types of businesses; (2) the method must be reasonably objective, that is, the rate cannot depend on someone's unverifiable judgment; and (3) the calculation must be relatively straightforward. Several possibilities are discussed here. Although further research and discussion is clearly necessary, the tentative conclusion is that the most feasible approach is:

1. Companies should calculate the interest cost of debt capital in the same manner they do now.

2. For financial reporting purposes, all companies should use an interest rate on equity capital that is either specified directly by the Financial Accounting Standards Board or that is arrived at objectively by a method prescribed by the FASB. This rate should represent a minimum equity interest cost; that is, it should be somewhat lower than the average cost of equity capital. It might be called the *prime equity rate*.

3. The rate applied to equity capital could be either the current rate or the rate that existed at the time that increment of capital was acquired, as is currently the case in calculating the interest cost of debt capital; however, it is unlikely that the prime equity rate will fluctuate much, if at all, from one year to the next.

It will be noted that this approach contains alternatives. The merits of each alternative are discussed in chapter 6. At this stage, the only significant point is that feasible, objective approaches do exist.

Accounting Procedures

If one accepts the fundamental proposition that interest is a cost, to be treated as other elements of cost are treated, most of the accounting procedures can be easily determined by analogy with other cost elements. They are described in chapter 7 and summarized below.

1. Each company should develop an overall interest rate. This rate should be the weighted average of its debt rate and its prime equity rate in a given year.

2. Except in those unusual situations in which there is a special mix of debt and equity capital, this overall rate should be applied to the capital employed for various cost objectives so as to determine the interest cost applicable to these cost objectives. Specifically,

a. the interest cost of capital assets used in the manufacturing process should be assigned to products in the same way that depreciation on plant and equipment is assigned;

b. the cost of self-constructed plant and equipment should include the interest cost of the capital assets used to construct the plant and equipment and the interest cost of other capital that is tied up during construction; and

c. the cost of acquired plant and equipment should include the interest cost of advance payments and progress payments.

3. Any interest cost for a year that is not assigned to cost objectives should be treated as a general expense of the year.

4. The credits for the above charges will be made in an *interest pool* account. This account will be debited for:

a. the actual cost of debt interest, adjusted for the tax effect of debt interest; and

b. the amount of equity interest, calculated at the prime equity rate.

5. The amount of equity interest should be credited to retained earnings.

Suggestions for Transition

The change proposed here is substantial, has many ramifications, and requires an extensive educational process before its import will be well understood. For these reasons, some way should be developed for making a gradual transition to the new method. Of the various possibilities for a piecemeal approach, starting with selected items in specific industries is perhaps the most attractive. Some suggestions are:

1. Include interest as an element of inventory cost in companies that hold inventory for long periods of time, such as the standing timber of lumber companies, the oil reserves of petroleum companies, and the inventories of tobacco, distilled liquor, and other products that are aged for several years.

2. Include interest as an element of cost in self-constructed buildings and equipment. This practice is already followed by public utility companies, and it is simple to extend it to all companies.

Conclusion

Although there is general acceptance of the fact that interest is an element of cost, the tendency is to dismiss rather quickly the idea that this cost should be recorded in the accounts, on the grounds that it is not feasible to do so and that even if it were feasible, the effort would not be worthwhile. This book argues that the idea is both feasible and beneficial.

I seek the support of theoreticians, but, more important, I hope that practical businessmen will become convinced of the merits of this proposal and urge the Financial Accounting Standards Board to adopt it.

2

Conceptual Foundations

This chapter discusses how the proposal relates to basic concepts in both economics and accounting. It demonstrates that the proposal to treat interest as a cost is consistent with the principles of economics, whereas present financial accounting practice is inconsistent with these principles. The proposal is also consistent with two fundamental concepts of financial accounting: the entity concept and the cost concept. The proposal does involve giving accounting recognition to an "imputed cost," but, in fact, financial accounting increasingly recognizes such costs. The proposal is also consistent with practices that many businesses follow in the accounting that they do as an aid to management.

The history of the treatment of interest in accounting is also described.

Economic Theory and Accounting

Economists refer to the "factors of production," usually listed as labor, natural resources, and capital. Each of these factors has a cost. The cost of using labor represents the amount necessary to induce employees to supply their personal services. The cost of using capital represents the amount necessary to induce investors to supply capital to the business. A company obtains capital from two sources, from lenders and from shareholders. Capital received from lenders is called debt capital or borrowed capital, and capital received from shareholders is called equity capital. In economics, interest is the cost of using *both* debt capital and equity capital.

Profit is the difference between revenue and the sum of all costs; that is, no profit is earned until all costs, including interest, are covered. A widely used economics text states the prevailing view:

The cost of a product means all the expenses necessary to induce producers to bring it to market. Over the long run this must include a normal rate of profit to the owners of the enterprise. Normal profit is in fact not profit at all. It is a necessary interest return on the owners' investment required to induce them to devote their funds to this line of production instead of do something else.

Profit is the difference between the actual return and the normal rate.[1]

Economists differ about where to draw the line between interest and profits. Some maintain that interest cost should take into account the risks

11

and uncertainties associated with a given investment, while others believe that risks and uncertainties are more properly considered as one of the factors that explain the amount of earned profit. This difference of opinion complicates the problem of measuring the cost of interest, but nevertheless, a satisfactory and practical solution to this problem does exist.

Financial Accounting Concepts

Financial accounting is supposed to measure and report the economic realities of a business: the assets controlled by a business, the sources of the capital used to acquire these assets, and the flow of resources into and out of the business. Accounting measurements cannot be completely consistent with the principles of economics, primarily because certain of these principles conflict with the fundamental requirement that accounting measurements be reasonably objective. Economics states, for example, that the value of a business is the present value of the stream of future earnings that the business will generate, but an estimate of this amount is so highly subjective that accountants do not attempt to record it for financial accounting purposes. Nevertheless, financial accounting should not be at variance with economics unless there is a compelling reason.

Financial accounting does not recognize the interest cost of equity capital at all, and in measuring the cost of manufactured products, financial accounting does not include the interest cost of either debt capital or of equity capital. Accountants give very little thought, however, to this difference between financial accounting and economics. They state flatly that their practices are "in accordance with generally accepted accounting principles," and that the recording of interest (except for the interest on debt capital) is *not*. This conclusion is unwarranted. Two basic financial accounting concepts do support the recording of interest as a cost. They are the entity concept and the cost concept.

The Entity Concept

In the nineteenth century, accounting was governed by what is called the *proprietary* concept. Most businesses were managed by their proprietors; there were few public corporations, that is, companies whose equity capital was furnished by outside investors.[2] Under the proprietary concept, assets are considered to be owned by the proprietors, and liabilities are considered the liabilities of the proprietors. This was legally the situation in unincorporated businesses, and it was considered the de facto situation in corporations owned by one person or one family. With such a concept, it was pointless to record as a separate number the cost of using equity capital. Rather, the important problem was to separate the interest of creditors, who were the only truly outside parties, from those of the proprietors. Profit was whatever remained after the claims of outsiders had been satisfied. Thus, it was important to measure the interest cost of debt capital, but not the interest cost of equity capital.

With the development of publicly owned corporations and, more recently, the development of the idea of corporate social responsibility, the basic thrust of accounting shifted from the proprietary concept to the entity concept. The rationale and consequences of this shift have been well described:

The break-through in accounting thought on the nature of the accounting entity can be traced back to the early 1930s when the question of the proper accounting entity became a topic of theoretical discussion. At issue was the question of whether the accounting entity should be defined in terms of the entity theory or in terms of the proprietary theory. According to the entity theory, the assets belong to the entity and the liabilities and equities represent sources of the assets, whether in the form of capital stock, a note payable, or any other type of equity. Even when equities are viewed as claims to assets rather than sources of assets, the entity theory is still a valid concept.

According to the proprietary theory, the assets of the enterprise are owned effectively by the stockholders and the liabilities are considered as liabilities of the stockholders. In the case of the sole proprietorship and the partnership, the proprietorship theory is pretty much in accordance with the legal facts of the situation. Partners and proprietors may well have to pay business liabilities out of personal assets if the business cannot pay them. Legally the debts of the business are a liability of the partners or proprietors and the assets of the business really belong to the partners or proprietors.

In the case of the corporation, however, the legal facts of the situation support the entity theory. The stockholders of the corporation assume no liability for the debts of the corporation and cannot withdraw assets from the corporation without corporate approval and action.

The view that the business organization is an entity separate and distinct from the owners of the business has influenced greatly the development of accounting. It has allowed for the extension of double entry accounting to cover transactions between the business and the owners. Overall it seems appropriate to suggest that the entity concept has contributed much to the rather amazing growth of accounting as a technique for collecting and recording basic business data in a systematic manner.[3]

Under the entity concept, the corporation is viewed as an entity separated from its proprietors. The entity obtains its capital from two principal sources: it obtains debt capital from creditors and equity capital from shareholders. Management decides on the best mix between debt capital and equity capital. Equity capital, therefore, becomes just another source of funds. Both creditors and equity investors are viewed as outsiders. The decision on whether to raise additional capital from creditors or from shareholders (either from the sale of shares or by retaining earnings) turns essentially on the balance between the risk and cost characteristics of these two sources of capital.

Under these circumstances, it would seem appropriate to measure the cost of using equity capital, which is supplied by outside shareholders, just as it is appropriate to measure the cost of using debt capital, which is also furnished by outside parties. From the standpoint of the entity, each type of capital is a resource furnished by an outside party. This, however, is not now done in accounting. The reasons why it is not done will be discussed in the next section.[4]

The entity concept conceivably could be used to assert that neither debt interest nor equity interest should be recorded as a cost in accounting. In such an accounting system, income would be the total amount available to both creditors and equity investors, and debt interest and dividends on common stock would be viewed as a distribution of income to creditors and shareholders, respectively. Those who support such an approach argue that information on business operations should be reported separately from information on how those operations are financed. Whatever the merits of this theory in relation to the *entity* concept, it clearly is inconsistent with the *cost* concept. Implementation of such a theory would move accounting even further away from economics than it now is, and I do not discuss this possibility further.

The Cost Concept

Financial accounting records costs. Assets are ordinarily recorded at their cost, and income is the difference between revenues and expenses, which are the costs associated with those revenues. Thus, interest should be recorded in the accounts if—but only if—interest is truly a cost.

Accounting Terminology Bulletin No. 4 contains a widely used definition of cost: "Cost is the amount, measured in money, of cash expended or other property transferred, capital stock issued, services performed or a liability incurred, in consideration of goods or services received or to be received." This definition is satisfactory as far as it goes, but it does not make entirely clear that cost always refers to the cost of *something*; this "something" is technically called a *cost objective*. For example, the cost of a building is the total amount of the resources used to acquire the building. This amount is represented by cash if the building is purchased, or by the sum of labor, material, and other resources if the building is constructed by the company itself. Similarly, the cost of a product is measured by the amount of cash expended or liability incurred if the product is purchased, and it is measured by the sum of labor, material, and other resources if the product is manufactured by the company.

Thus, cost measures the amount of resources used for a cost objective. In manufacturing a product, a company uses labor, measured by labor costs; it uses material, measured by material costs; and it uses services, measured by utility costs, rentals, and similar items. The appropriate amount of cost for each resource is not always easy to measure. The cost of personal services, for example, includes not only wages and salaries earned by employees, but the associated fringe benefits as well. One of these fringe benefits may be the right to a future pension, and it is difficult to estimate the current cost of providing for pensions that will be paid some years hence. Despite the difficulties, such estimates are made, and accounting principles set forth fairly detailed guidelines for making them.

A business also uses capital; that is, it obtains funds that it uses to acquire assets. It obtains this capital from two principal sources, lenders and shareholders. Lenders will not furnish debt capital to a company unless they expect to receive a reward for doing so. This reward, called interest, is the cost of the use of debt capital. The equity capital obtained from shareholders also has a cost. Investors will not furnish equity capital to a company unless they expect to receive a reward for doing so, and this reward is the cost of the use of equity capital. To the business entity, this cost is as real as the cost of the use of debt capital.

The amount of the expected reward for the use of equity capital is less clearly identifiable than that for the use of debt capital. Those who provide debt capital expect an amount that is labelled interest. Those who provide equity capital expect a reward that is the sum of two amounts: (1) dividends and (2) an appreciation in the market value of their shares. They do not expect that dividends alone will be an adequate reward; rather, they anticipate that some of the earnings that result from their investment will be retained by the corporation and that the profits generated by these retained earnings, as well as other factors, will cause an appreciation in market value. The fact that the reward expected by an equity investor takes these two separate forms does not alter the conclusion that equity capital does have a cost and that this cost is related to the reward that equity investors expect when they furnish their capital to the business.

Unfortunately, accounting has no generally agreed on term for the cost of using equity capital. This is part of the problem. *Dividends* is not the correct term because, as noted above, shareholders in most companies expect that their total return will be greater than the current dividend yield, and that they will receive this portion of the return in the form of a higher market value when they sell their shares. The fact that the average dividend yield is only about 3 percent, as compared with rates for debt interest of 8 percent or more, proves this fairly obvious point.[5] The amount of current dividends is therefore an understatement of the cost of equity capital.

Profit and *net income* are also incorrect terms for the cost of using equity capital. Net income measures a company's performance; it is not itself a cost, but rather represents the difference between expired cost (i.e., expense) and revenue. In the present financial accounting structure, net income *includes* the cost of using equity capital, but it is not equated to that cost. Net income also includes the rewards for superior management, a superior product, a superior market position, and so on.

Although no specific term in accounting covers the cost of using equity capital, there is no need to invent one. Accountants can follow economists and use *interest* as the term for the cost of using either type of capital—debt capital or equity capital. This would emphasize the similarity of the *use* of both types of capital. Once capital has been acquired, a dollar of equity capital is the same as a dollar of debt capital. A business does not use debt capital to pay some its bills and equity capital to pay the remainder. It pays its bills with cash; and each dollar of cash is like every other dollar.

An analogy to employees helps to make this point. If a company fills one position with Employee A, who was hired from the outside, but fills another position with Employee B, who was promoted from within, the difference in the source of the labor service does not affect the cost of the labor service. If the services of Employee A cost $15,000 and those of Employee B cost $17,000, it is appropriate to call these amounts the labor cost of each employee, without regard to the difference in source. Similarly, we can refer to the interest cost of capital employed, without regard to the source of the capital. When it is desirable to specify the source as being equity capital, we can use the phrase "equity interest," just as we now use "bond interest," "debt interest," "note interest," and similar terms.

Alternative terms, such as the *cost of capital employed* or the *cost of using capital* would also be descriptive. They have the advantage of suggesting, correctly, that we seek to measure the cost of *using* capital for various cost objectives, but they have the disadvantage of being longer terms than *interest*.

Interest Cost Versus Profit

Since accountants customarily use the word *interest* only with reference to the cost of debt capital, the broader definition suggested here requires some getting used to. More important, there are both conceptual and practical problems in measuring the new kind of interest, that is, interest on equity capital. The conceptual problems are discussed here, and the practical problems will be deferred to chapter 6.

Net income, as currently defined, is the algebraic sum of two components, equity interest and profit. (The profit component can be either positive or negative.) In order to measure equity interest cost, we must somehow separate the interest component from the profit component. The principal conceptual problem in making such a separation has to do with the treatment of risk.

Equity investors expect a higher total return on their money than do bondholders because they assume more risks then do bondholders. Other than in special situations, such as when the objective is to gain control, a rational person who has the choice of a legally binding return of 8 percent on a bond issue or an expected, but not legally binding return of 8 percent on a stock issue in the same company would select the former. A rational person would invest in stocks only if the expected return was greater than 8 percent. Furthermore, equity investors in speculative companies expect a higher return than they would expect from a seasoned "blue chip" company, because the risk in the speculative company is greater.

Conceptually, the problem is whether this reward for risk is more appropriately assigned to the interest component or to the profit component of net income. There are two schools of thought on this question. The first maintains that interest cost should reflect differences in risk, and the second holds that interest cost should measure only the "pure" cost of capital, and that the extra rewards for risk should show up in the profit component of net income.

The current treatment of debt interest corresponds to the first school of thought. Some companies can borrow at the prime rate, while others must pay one, two, or even more percentage points above prime. This variation is associated with the riskiness of the individual company and is to be distinguished from variations in the average cost of various types of debt —long versus short term, secured versus unsecured, convertible versus nonconvertible, and so on. In measuring the cost of debt capital, we make no attempt to separate the pure interest element from the risk element of the total charge; the whole amount is called interest.

If the same approach were used for equity capital, then clearly the equity interest rate would vary with the riskiness and uncertainties of particular investments. Among other reasons, it would be higher in certain industries than in others, and higher for highly leveraged companies than for companies with relatively little debt. With this approach, the profit residual would measure a company's ability to earn more than the amount required as a compensation for risk, for reasons such as excellent management, excellent products or market position, excellent economic conditions, excellent production facilities, or luck. In an average year, the average company would report zero profit.

Such an approach to the measurement of the cost of equity capital would be difficult to implement. Although there is general agreement that the equity interest rate is lowest in regulated companies, higher in seasoned companies in stable industries, and highest in young companies in cyclical industries, there is no agreement at all on how these differences should be measured. Indeed, there is not even agreement on what constitutes a "cyclical industry" or how a given company that operates in several industries should be classified.

The alternative approach is to define equity interest cost as a "pure" cost of equity capital. The additional return that is required by equity investors in risky situations would then be part of the profit component, rather than part of the interest component. The equity interest rate might be higher than the prime interest rate, to reflect the fact that equity investments are inherently riskier than debt investments, but the equity interest rate would not vary with the riskiness of specific equity investments. Under this approach, reported profits would be higher than under the first approach. Although the second approach involves a single *equity* interest rate, the interest rate on *total* capital employed would vary among companies, because companies have different debt interest rates and different mixes of debt and equity.

The principal argument for the first approach, in which the equity intrest rate varies with the company's risk, is that it is symmetrical with the way in which debt interest is treated. The principal argument for the second approach, in which all equity capital is costed at the same rate, is that it is much easier to implement. Unless further research demonstrates that a feasible way of measuring the risk component can be developed, the second approach seems preferable.

Some argue that an equity interest rate that does not include a risk component is meaningless, because the return expected by equity investors *does* vary with the riskiness of the investment. A more accurate conclusion is that such a rate has a *different* meaning than a rate that incorporates risk. The pure equity rate does permit a cost for the use of capital to be developed, with all the advantages discussed in chapters 3, 4, and 5. It would be a lower cost than that resulting from the incorporation of a risk component, and the profit residual would be correspondingly higher. Users of financial statements must understand this, but once they do understand it they can interpret the resulting numbers correctly.

Imputed Costs

Although few would assert that equity interest is not a cost, some argue that it is an imputed cost and that accounting does not record imputed costs. This is a slippery point, because there is no precise meaning in accounting for the term *imputed*. Kohler defines it as "a term often used to indicate the presence of arbitrary or subjective elements of product cost having more than usual significance; the worth of a factor of production joined with and inseparable from one or more other factors."[6] This definition, however, fails to capture what is actually practiced. Accountants do not record *some* "arbitrary or subjective" elements of cost, but they do record others. They do not record "opportunity costs," that is, the value of a resource as measured by its value in some alternative use; nor do they record those social costs that are not measured by actual company outlays, such as the cost to society of a company's pollution of the atmosphere or a river. These are imputed costs in the sense that no measurable transaction is associated with them.

On the other hand, accounting does record some types of cost for which no documented transaction exists. Under certain circumstances, a leased building or machine is recorded at its equivalent purchase cost although no record of this cost exists. If a company acquires a noncash asset in exchange for a note that either does not stipulate an interest rate or stipulates a rate that is clearly unreasonable, *APB Opinion No. 21* requires that the true interest component be estimated. As already noted, labor cost includes an estimate of the present value of future pension benefits, and although this estimate is dignified with the word "actuarial," neither the actuary nor anyone else knows what the correct amount is. Allowances for bad debts, for the the future cost of warranty agreements, and for writedown of inventories to market are estimates, not based on documented transactions. In short, the argument that financial accounting deals only with "transacted" costs is not supported by actual practice.

Imputed costs are not synonymous with noncash costs. The depreciation expense in a given year is a noncash cost. Although the cost of the depreciable asset itself is usually measured by a cash outlay, the amount of this cost assigned as a depreciation expense in a single year is an estimate, not substantiated by an arm's length, or any other kind of transaction. Fifty years ago, this was used as an argument against recording depreciation; today, everyone agrees that it is better to be "approximately right than entirely wrong." It is better to make an estimate of depreciation expense than to omit this cost on the grounds that the amount cannot be measured precisely. Similarly, most of the examples given in the preceding paragraph do not involve a determinable cash outlay as of the time the events occur. The amount of cash that eventually will be involved is an estimate. In the case of donated assets, even depreciation is not tied to a cash transaction.

In general, the argument that accounting does not record imputed costs is valid only if imputed costs are defined as those costs that accounting has decided not to record. This circular argument is not very useful.

A more accurate conclusion from the examples given above is that accounting records items of cost that can be measured or estimated in some reasonable way. Equity interest meets this criterion (chapter 6).

Objectivity

A basic criterion of financial accounting is that the information should be reasonably objective; that is, it should not be biased by subjective judgments. The amounts should be verifiable, in the sense that they "would be substantially duplicated by independent measurers using the same measurement methods."[7] This does not mean that accounting information must be precise; amounts for depreciation and many other items of cost are based on estimates of an unknowable future. The proposal for recording equity interest as a cost fully meets the criterion of objectivity (chapter 6).

Realization

I shall conclude this discussion of relevant accounting concepts by referring to the realization concept, because some critics have argued that the proposal to record equity interest violates this concept. The realization concept is, basically, that revenue is not recognized in the accounts until the period in which the revenue is realized, usually by an arm's length sales transaction. Critics point out that the recording of equity interest as a cost would involve an offsetting credit to retained earnings or to some other shareholders' equity account, and that when the cost is locked up in an unsold inventory or unamortized plant account, shareholders' equity is increased prior to a realized sales transaction.

This criticism could be countered by pointing out that the realization concept relates to revenue, not to shareholders' equity as such, and that the measurement of revenue is completely unaffected by the proposal. Such a counter, however, does not deal with the basic idea that lies behind the realization concept, namely, that profits should not be anticipated.

In my view, the proposal does *not* involve an anticipation of profits. Those who argue to the contrary fail to make the necessary distinction between net income as it is currently defined and as it would be defined under the procedures proposed here. Under the proposed treatment, net income would be the amount left over after accounting for the cost of using capital. The credit entry for equity interest arises in accounting for this item of cost. There would be no overstatement of shareholders' equity, no anticipation of profit, *unless* the inclusion of interest in asset amounts caused these amounts to exceed the net realizable value of the assets. This would happen only in unusual circumstances, and when it did happen, any overstatement should be avoided by writing inventory down to market value, just as is done in other circumstances in which cost exceeds market.

An Historical Note

Proposals to record total interest cost (that is, both debt interest and equity interest) were first advanced many years ago, and interest has been recorded outside the formal accounts in certain situations. A brief review of history may be instructive.

The first recognition of total interest cost in the United States coincided with the beginning of utility regulation, the formation of public utility commissions in New York and Wisconsin in the 1870s. Rates were set so as to provide a fair rate of return on the capital employed. Even in early court cases involving utility regulations, a distinction was made between interest, or the cost of this capital, and profit. The landmark case of *Hill* v. *Antigo Water Co.* noted: "Interest arises from the use of capital, and profits have their source in business ability, skill, and foresight in management, as well as in the risks assumed by it or by the entrepreneur." The decision continued, "Interest is justifiable because of the importance of capital in production, and necessary because without it capital cannot be had for industrial and commercial purposes."[8] In this decision, no distinction was made between debt capital and equity capital.

From about 1910 to the mid-1920s, a return on invested capital was counted as a cost in reports prepared by members of some trade associations, including grocery stores, department stores, and shoe and leather companies. Those responsible for designing such reports recognized that the operating results of different companies would not be comparable unless allowances were made for differences between companies that used their own capital to buy fixed assets and companies that used rented facilities. The Harvard Research Bureau, from 1913 through 1924, included a charge for interest in various studies that it made, on the grounds that no business was really profitable until interest costs were met. Its director wrote, in 1916:

The Bureau has come to the conclusion that every business, whether or not incorporated, should bear a specific charge for interest on the net investment—the amount which capital could earn if invested elsewhere. No business is truly profitable unless it yields the proprietor not only a salary for his time and rent for his store, if he owns it, but also interest on this investment. The Bureau has decided, furthermore, that it is more practicable from an accounting standpoint to consider this interest charge a part of expense rather than a distribution of profit.[9]

The Federal Trade Commission also supported this view of interest.

In its "Fundamentals of a Cost System for Manufacturers'" the following appeared:

Rent includes a return on the investment so when it is desired to make comparisons between plants where the building is owned and where it is rented, the return on the investment must be taken into consideration. It is desirable to include interest in cost where it is desired to show the effect of variations in the amount of capital employed and the term of employment. It is impossible to get true relative costs unless consideration is given to interest on the capital employed.[10]

The Interdepartmental Conference on Uniform Contracts and Cost Accounting Definitions and Methods, formed during World War I for the purpose of defining uniform accounting practices for government war contracts, issued an advisory in 1917 which stated that "interest, rent, and selling expenses will not be allowed as part of the overhead cost but may be the subject of special compensation when so stipulated in the contract." Many arms contracts did stipulate that interest was an allowable cost.

The courts have considered the invested capital question in companies other than public utilities. Between 1894 and 1918, there are records of decisions at all court levels through the US Supreme Court, both for and against the inclusion of interest, depending on the facts in specific cases. In allowing interest inclusion, the Court of Appeals for the Second Circuit, in an April 1918 decision, stated: "Certainly, a merchant cannot correctly determine what his profit is until he knows the amount of his investment together with interest thereon, whether the investment is made out of his own funds or borrowed capital."[11]

In the second and third decades of the twentieth century, a number of articles and books advocated the inclusion of interest on total capital as a cost. The entire April 1913 issue of the *Journal of Accountancy* was devoted to articles on this topic. Some of the points made then are as valid today. For example, William Morse Cole discussed the importance of allowing for interest on total capital in pricing decisions and in analyses of proposed investments (two of the topics discussed in chapter 5). He concluded:

We have seen that for analytical purposes, in studying operations, practical necessity requires us at least to consider interest in virtually all calculations when investment is involved; and we have seen that in financial statements practical convenience is served by the treatment of interest as a charge, or cost, rather than as a residue, or profit. It seems reasonable, therefore, for accountants to adopt a terminology that will serve their own ends, will agree with the terminology of economists, and will mislead no one. Business men are likely to be misled in the future, as they have been in the past, by statements of profit which assume that no cost is involved in the use of capital.[12]

Cole's conclusion, written sixty years ago, is a good summary of the argument made here.

In the period 1920 through 1926, the *Accountant's Index* listed over two hundred references on the topic of interest as a cost. The American Association of University Instructors in Accounting (predecessor of the American Accounting Association) devoted a session at one of its annual meetings to the subject. The American Institute of Accountants (predecessor of the American Institute of CPAs) appointed a special committee, which reported: "The inclusion in production cost of interest on investment is unsound in theory and wrong, not to say absurd, in practice."[13] And William A. Paton, in his 1922 doctoral dissertation, declined to discuss the possibility of including interest as a cost on the grounds that the topic was "long since worn threadbare by disputation."[14]

Perhaps the most influential advocate of recording interest during the first decades of the century was C.H. Scovell, founder of a prominent public accounting firm.[15] After his death in 1927, serious discussion faded away. For example, the important report *Changing Concepts of Business Income*, prepared in 1952 by a committee of forty-four prominent accountants, businessmen, economists, and lawyers, did not even address the question of whether interest on equity capital is a cost, although statements from economists along the lines reported earlier in this chapter were included in the background material.[16]

The subject continued to be treated in some textbooks as a topic of academic, but not practical, importance. The second edition of Schlatter and Schlatter's *Cost Accounting* had a whole chapter on "Interest as a Cost of Manufacturing."[17] Some current texts continue to discuss the topic briefly, but most do not mention it.[18] As an exception, Bierman's *Theory* text does recommend recognition of interest in accounting for accretion, such as in timber, and in construction.[19] In contrast, Welsch, Zlatkovich, and White state flatly that, with respect to public utility plant, "Capitalization of interest during the construction period is not theoretically sound and should not be permitted."[20]

In their *Accounting Research Study No. 3*, Sprouse and Moonitz approach the subject indirectly. They state as their first principle: "Profit is attributable to the whole process of business activity."[21] They recommend that inventory be measured at net realizable value and point out, "This procedure will have the result of assigning most if not all of the change in resources and the related profit or loss to the period of production (or other activity) when the actual effort was made." This contrasts with current practice, in which the entire return to the shareholders is recognized at the time of sale. Inclusion of equity interest as an element of cost would also assign at least some of what is currently counted as the profit to the period of production. The Moonitz and Sprouse proposal, therefore, would arrive at roughly the same end result as that proposed here, but by a different route.

Current Status in Financial Accounting

In a recent position paper, the Management Accounting Practices Committee, which is authorized to speak for the National Association of Accountants, rejected the idea of capitalizing interest.[22] Some authors mention the inclusion of interest cost as part of a proposal for making fundamental changes in the approach to accounting.[23] Professor Kenneth S. Most has called my attention to a recent British book that does advocate the inclusion of interest as a cost.[24]

From 1959 until 1973, the principal source of financial accounting standards in the United States was the Accounting Principles Board of the American Institute of Certified Public Accountants (APB). No Opinion, Statement, or Research Study of the APB discussed the possibility of including interest on capital employed as an element of cost. A member of the board, with one of his colleagues, did prepare a working paper on the topic, but it was never placed on the board's agenda.[25]

In a notable exception to the prevailing views, Philip L. Defliese, managing partner of Coopers & Lybrand, has recommended the recognition of interest cost, both debt and equity interest, in order to make the accounting for purchased assets consistent with that for leased assets. His proposal is basically similar to that made here and will be described in later chapters.[26]

In its 1973 pronouncement on Accounting for Retail Land Sales, the AICPA (but not the APB) indicated its acceptance of capitalization of interest on land inventory.

In public utility accounting, interest on capital is included as an element of cost in assets constructed by the public utility. Interest "includes the net cost of borrowed funds used for construction purposes and a reasonable rate upon the utility's own funds when so used."[27]

Professor Bonbright explains the use of a "reasonable rate" in the above rule:

As to the question whether the allowance for interest during construction should be based on percentage rates approximating contract interest on secure loans, or whether it should be based on a higher rate approximating an accepted "fair rate of return" the well-recognized market preference for early, and hence less uncertain, realization strongly suggests a time discount not lower than that reflected by a standard "fair rate of return."[28]

Public utilities are motivated to include interest as a cost because it adds to the asset base on which their allowable rates are calculated.

Debt interest, but usually not equity interest, is included as an element of cost, and hence capitalized, in certain long-term construction projects, for motion picture and television films, and for similar projects that require tying up significant amounts of capital for substantial periods of time. Of six hundred industrial and commercial companies whose 1971 financial statements were analyzed in *Accounting Trends and Techniques*, twenty-one mentioned the capitalization of interest on some asset, in most cases a major construction project. [29] The Securities and Exchange Commission, however, has moved to stop this practice until the Financial Accounting Standards Board has acted on the question of interest as a cost.[30]

Thus, current practice is inconsistent. Public utilities include both debt and equity interest cost as a cost element in plants they construct. A few industrial companies include debt interest, but not equity interest, as an element of plant cost, especially when they use a construction loan specifically for the project. Most companies do not include interest as an element of cost. For those companies that do include interest as a cost, the amount of cost varies with the proportion of debt financing in the project. Thus, for a $100 million project (excluding interest) requiring three years to complete, the recorded cost could be $100 million for a company that does not count interest as a cost, perhaps $105 million for a company that records debt interest and uses 50 percent debt financing, or perhaps more than $110 million for a public utility or a company that uses debt financing primarily. These differences are not trivial; in 1970 the capitalized interest by utilities amounted to 19 percent of their net income.[31] It seems illogical that the cost of an asset should be a function of the method of paying for it.

Management Accounting

Although interest on total capital is rarely recorded as a cost in financial accounting—that is, in the preparation of financial statements for the use of investors and other external parties—the concept that the use of capital does have a cost is well accepted in accounting done for internal use, as an aid to management. The cost of using capital is recognized in many situations, the three principal ones being capital investment decisions, pricing, and the measurement of divisional performance.

Capital Investment Decisions

A relatively new but widely accepted technique in analyzing a proposed capital acquisition includes among the relevant costs not only the cost of the asset itself, but also a return on the capital used to acquire the asset. Such a return corresponds to interest in the sense used in this book. Books and articles recommending the use of present values, or discounting techniques, or a specific capital charge in such calculations appeared in the early decades of the twentieth century, but these methods were not widely used by businesses until the 1950s. They are now used by most well-informed managers (although they are not used in all capital investment proposals because some proposals are not susceptible to quantitative analysis). There is general agreement today that such formerly popular techniques as the "payback method" or "the accounting method," which do not incorporate a return on capital employed, are not generally valid. The widespread recognition of the validity of the cost-of-capital concept is only twenty years old. Perhaps its newness explains the failure of financial accountants to recognize it formally.

Pricing

As far back as 1927, an article describing the pricing practices of General Motors stated that a return on capital employed was an explicit component of the price calculation.[32] At that time the practice of making an explicit allowance for such a return was relatively uncommon. Today, in arriving at selling prices, a great many companies do take into account the amount of capital employed when it is relevant; that is, they no longer price so as to achieve the same percentage margin on sales for all products if their various products require the use of different amounts of capital. Supermarkets have a lower profit margin on sales than do jewelry stores, primarily because supermarkets use a lower amount of capital per sales dollar. The name of the game is return on capital employed, not return on sales.

Although this concept is familiar to businessmen, only recently has it been accepted by the US Department of Defense for pricing cost-type contracts, and currently it is used only on an experimental basis. Until the 1960s, most Department of Defense contracts were priced so that the contractor could expect to recover his costs plus a fee that was calculated as a percentage of the estimated cost. In 1961, Secretary of Defense Robert S. McNamara instituted a thorough reexamination of contract-pricing practices. In the course of this review, some people proposed that the basis of calculating the fee, or profit, be shifted from a percentage of estimated cost to a percentage of capital employed. The proposal was shot down, largely because of a memorandum by Joel Dean, an eminent economist, who judged it to be impractical, although acknowledging its theoretical merit.

A number of studies in the middle and late 1960s highlighted the defects of the percentage-of-cost approach, and in the late 1960s pilot tests in hundreds of actual contracts demonstrated the feasibility of calculating a return on capital employed. These studies were not received enthusiastically, however. Because several large defense contractors had found ways to minimize the amount of capital employed on defense contracts, they were able to earn a large return on capital employed, although their profit as a percentage of costs was low. A return-on-capital approach would result in a lower fee for such companies, and consequently they opposed this approach. Although their opposition has delayed the shift to a return-on-capital approach in the United States, the deputy secretary of defense did nonetheless approve the policy in July 1971, and the return-on-capital approach was used on a few contracts beginning in 1973.

In setting selling prices for its uranium enrichment services, which in 1973 amounted to $514 million, the Atomic Energy Commission included interest on its invested capital as an element of cost. The amount for 1973 was $66 million.[33]

The appraised value of property is a type of price that is important in many transactions. Appraisers often arrive at the value of an asset by estimating the present value of the future benefits to be derived from it. This is a widely used method for appraising public utility and public service property and is recommended authoritatively for all types of income producing real property.[34] Such an approach implicitly takes account of the interest cost of using capital because the rate at which the stream of future benefits is discounted corresponds to the interest rate.

Measuring Divisional Performance

In measuring the profitablility of a division or other profit center within a company, a method that incorporates both profits and assets employed is more inclusive, and thus better, than a method that measures profits only. If Divisions A and B each earn $1 million and if Division A has half the assets of Division B, Division A is making a greater contribution to the overall well-being of the company. A great many companies, therefore, do incorporate assets employed in their system for measuring divisional performance.

The fact that many companies include interest as a cost in divisional performance measurement is highly significant, on two counts. First, it shows that the procedure is feasible. Second, it shows that management finds the practice to be useful; otherwise the company would not operate an internal performance measurement system that has different principles from those required for financial reporting purposes, for such a system both involves extra recordkeeping and also sets up an inconsistency between internal reports and external reports. As we shall see in chapter 3, some people argue that readers of published financial statements can make mental allowances for the fact that interest is not accounted for as a cost and therefore do not need an explicit recognition of this cost in the statements. If management, much more familiar with the business than any outside analyst can be, finds the explicit recognition of interest useful, it seems unlikely that outsiders can safely rely on mental adjustments to the reported numbers.

Summary

Economists regard interest on total capital, both debt and equity, as an element of cost. Accountants, however, record only the interest cost of debt capital. Accounting practice is consistent with the proprietary concept of accounting, which was dominant in the nineteenth century, but the inclusion of equity interest as a cost is consistent with the entity concept, which underlies current thinking.

There is a cost in using equity capital, and recording this cost in the accounts is consistent with the concept of cost, a fundamental accounting principle. Some argue that it is only an "imputed" cost, but other kinds of imputed costs are nevertheless recorded in the accounts.

Early in the twentieth century, several authorities advocated the inclusion of total interest in the accounts, and the practice was followed in various special studies, in war contracts, in public utility rate regulation, and in various court decisions. However, the practice was not generally adopted.

In information prepared as a basis of management decisions—for capital acquisition decisions, for pricing decisions, and for the measurement of divisional performance—it is increasingly common to recognize the cost of using capital; that is, explicitly to allow for interest. Management finds such information useful. In these calculations, no distinction is ordinarily drawn between the cost of using debt capital and the cost of using equity capital; the relevant amount is the interest cost of the total capital employed.

3 Implications for Financial Reporting

Recording interest as a cost would have two types of effects on financial statements. First, the amounts reported for certain asset items would be higher because of the inclusion of interest as an element of the cost of these assets, and the shareholders' equity would be correspondingly higher. Second, the amount of net income would be lower because of the treatment of equity interest as an element of cost rather then as an element of net income. Of these two effects, the tendency is to focus on the second because of the dramatically different amount reported for net income. Actually, the first effect has a more fundamental significance. If it were not that asset amounts would be significantly changed, the proposal could be described as merely a separation of the conventional net income amount into two components, interest and profit. We shall therefore discuss the effect on asset amounts first.

This chapter also discusses objections that have been made to the proposal insofar as it relates to financial accounting.

Balance Sheet Effects

The amounts reported for two types of assets—inventory and plant— would be increased by the recording of interest. The increase in inventory would result from either or both of two circumstances: (1) the cost of inventories that are held for significantly long periods of time would be increased by the interest cost associated with holding these inventories; and (2) inventory amounts of goods manufactured would be increased because of the inclusion, as an element of cost, of interest on the capital employed in the manufacturing process. The increase in plant would result from the inclusion of interest cost as an element of the cost of acquiring or building plant.

Inventory

The longer an item remains in inventory, the greater is its real cost to the company because of the cost of the capital that is tied up in it. As far back as 1912, Professor Theodore Limperg called attention to the strange ways that

29

accountants reckoned the cost of a Steinway concert piano. The wood in such a piano comes from an inventory that has dried and mellowed for perhaps a hundred years. During all those years, Steinway had a considerable investment locked up in that inventory, but the accountants' definition of cost completely disregards the consequences of this use of capital. The accountant says that the wood in a Steinway costs the same as, or even less than, the wood used in furniture constructed from timber that has just been cut.[1]

The omission of interest cost from inventories also results in a misleading impression of what is actually happening to the shareholders' equity. Consider, for example, a corporation that is formed to invest in land. It buys a parcel of land for $1,000,000, holds it for five years, sells the land for $2,000,000 at the end of the fifth year, and liquidates. (We shall disregard property taxes, debt interest, and other operating costs, in order to focus on the consequences of alternative treatments of equity interest. If the reader is uncomfortable with this simplifying assumption, he can assume that the land produces rental income in an amount that just equals these costs.) According to convential accounting, the financial statements would report that the shareholders' equity remained unchanged during the first four years in which the land was held, and that it took a big jump in the fifth year; that is, the statements would indicate that the company's performance was poor in each of the first four years and that it suddenly became good in the fifth year. Actually, this company's performance may well have been exactly as its investors had contemplated when they formed it. They were willing to invest in the land because they expected, over the whole period, to earn a return on their investment. To report that their investment is unchanged during the first four years and that it suddenly increases when the land is sold is misleading.

In the proposed system, interest cost would be added to the cost of the land each year, and there would be a corresponding credit to shareholders' equity. At the end of the fifth year, there would be an additional entry to shareholders' equity, representing the net income realized from the sale; that is, the difference between the sales revenue and the accumulated cost of the land. Thus, the statements would show an increase in shareholders' equity in each of the five years. During the first four years, the company would report neither income nor loss; instead, the costs incurred in holding the land, here assumed to be only equity interest, would be added to the original cost of the land. In the fifth year, when the sale took place, net income would be reported as the difference between the selling price and the costs accumulated in inventory up to that time.

Proponents of current practice argue that this treatment is not conservative, that the annual increase in shareholders' equity might lead the shareholders to conclude that they have made a profit in each of the first four years. This argument is not valid, because the income statements for these four years would not report a profit. In accordance with the realization concept, income would be reported only in the fifth year, when the land was sold. In the first four years, the statements would report an increase in the shareholders' investment, which is in fact what has happened; that is, by deciding to hold the land, the shareholders have tied up additional capital in it each year.

The effect of including interest on capital employed as an element of the cost of goods manufactured is fundamentally the same as that in the case of the land described above. Shareholders' equity would be increased by virtue of the equity interest charged to products manufactured, and this increase would take place during the period of manufacture. The effect would not be as dramatic as in the case of the land, of course, because of the shorter time period involved in the usual manufacturing process. As in the case of the land, net income would not be reported until the products are sold. Even so, shareholders' equity would be affected earlier in the production-marketing cycle than is the case in conventional accounting, because of the credit for equity interest that is made as production occurs.

The rationale for the inclusion of interest as an element of manufacturing cost is that the manufacturing process requires capital, this capital has a cost, the cost is incurred when the products are produced, and the date of their sale has nothing to do with it. If accounting treated interest as a cost of production, the way labor, material, and services are treated, it would merely be recognizing the economic realities.

In many companies the interest carrying cost is immaterial because inventory turns over frequently, but it is of considerable importance in companies that hold inventories for significantly long periods of time. Financial accounting does not recognize this cost, and as a result, it understates the cost of such inventories. The importance of measuring the economic realities of inventory and other assets held for future sale will be discussed briefly for timber, petroleum and other mineral reserves, and products that age.

Timber. The accounts of most lumber companies do not show the cost associated with the use of capital to finance stands of timber. As a consequence of this practice, inventory amounts are understated, and net income does not conform to economic realities. Moreover, net income is significantly affected by choice of timber stands that are harvested in a given year. If timber is harvested from stands planted by the company or stands acquired as immature trees many years previously, the recorded profit is much higher than if the harvested timber came from stands purchased as mature trees. This is because the purchase of mature trees reflects the costs, including carrying costs, that were incurred by the former owner, while the cost of trees grown by the company does not. Thus, net income for a year is relatively high if there is a high proportion of cutting from stands whose recorded costs were low, and net income is relatively low if the mix of cutting is in the other direction. Since all the mature trees in a certain area have approximately the same value, regardless of whether they were grown or purchased, this variation in reported income makes no economic sense. If financial accounting recorded the fact that an interest cost was incurred for each year that the timberland was held in inventory, the discrepancy would be reduced.

Petroleum and Other Mineral Reserves. It is not unusual for a petroleum company to carry on its balance sheet, at their original cost, oil reserves that were discovered or purchased a generation earlier. The company had sound reasons for committing its capital to these reserves for a long period of time; it needs an assured source of supply in order to guarantee continued operations. Under present practice, no account is taken of the cost of committing this capital. The reserves remain on the balance sheet at, say, 25 cents a barrel, and on the day that the oil is sold, at perhaps $6.00 a barrel, financial accounting records that a gross profit of $5.75 has been earned. The total net income of the company in a given year is significantly influenced by what fields the oil was produced from in that year, since the older fields tend to have the lowest recorded cost. Companies that produce from reserves that were acquired at low cost a long time ago report higher profits than companies that produce from newly acquired reserves. As a matter of economic reality, the net income of some petroleum companies in a given year is significantly overstated, for no account is taken of the interest cost that has been incurred in holding reserves for a period of years. The same phenomenon operates in companies that have committed their capital to reserves of coal, stone, copper, lead, and other mineral resources.

In addition to its effect on the financial statements of individual companies, current practice misleads the public about the true cost of energy and of natural resources generally. Because interest cost is omitted, the reserves of these resources appear on the collective balance sheets of the companies that hold them at amounts far below their real cost. Since the reported net income overstates the true profit and since assets are stated less than cost, both the numerator and the denominator of the return on investment ratio in these companies is in error. The public criticism of these apparently high returns is not surprising. The apparently high returns are used by the press, by the Congress, and by many others as evidence that oil companies make unconscionable profits. In general, the true cost of energy is higher than the public realizes because the cost of carrying reserves is not included as an element of cost.

Aged inventories. Tobacco, distilled spirits, and certain wines are examples of products that must be aged for several years before they are sold. During the aging process, the manufacturer has significant amounts of capital committed to this inventory. In a very real sense, the longer the product remains in inventory, the more it costs. Since accounting does not recognize this element of cost, the inventory amounts of these companies are understated.

It should be emphasized that the proposal to include interest as an element of inventory cost is entirely consistent with the cost concept that currently governs the treatment of nonmonetary assets in financial accounting. By contrast, proposals that inventory should be measured at replacement value or at market value require a basic departure from the cost concept. The inclusion of interest as a cost would tend to bring reported inventory costs closer to replacement values, and therefore would move accounting in the direction that advocates of replacement value want it to go.

Plant. Except in public utilities, a building that is constructed by a company's own personnel appears in the financial accounts at a lower cost than an identical building constructed by an outside contractor. When a building is constructed by an outside contractor, he almost surely includes interest on his total capital in calculating his selling price; that is, he includes interest on his debt capital as a specific cost element, and he includes an allowance for profit which approximates the interest cost of his equity capital. The contractor's selling price becomes the buyer's cost. Interest is therefore a part of the cost of such a building. There is no logical reason why a building should cost less, by the omission of interest, if it is constructed by the company's own force. Furthermore, it makes no sense that a building constructed by a public utility should be recorded at a higher cost than an identical building constructed by an industrial company.

Similar incongruities arise when advance payments or progress payments are made in connection with the acquisition of assets. Airplanes, for example, are purchased under a variety of financing arrangements. At the two extremes, an airplane may be purchased by a payment of, say, $30 million in advance of construction, or it may be purchased by a payment of perhaps $33 million at the time of delivery. There are a variety of intermediate amounts depending on the schedule of progress payments. The differences solely reflect the interest cost. It is inconsistent to record the costs of physically identical aircraft at these varying amounts. If interest on advance payments and progress payments were recorded as a cost, these differences would disappear.

Leased Assets

If an asset is leased, rather than purchased, the lease payments almost surely include depreciation plus an element of interest—both debt and equity interest. Since the lease payment is a cost to the lessee, the lessee's cost for the use of the asset includes interest, whereas a company that purchases an identical asset reports only its depreciation as a cost. In other words, for the use of physically identical facilities, an owner records less annual cost than does a lessee.

Accountants have for several years tried to develop practices that would lessen this discrepancy. In 1964, APB *Opinion No. 5* took the approach that assets leased under certain types of financial lease agreements should be capitalized and accounted for as if they had been purchased; however, the requirements for capitalization were so narrowly defined that relatively few assets were affected. Up to its demise in 1973, the Accounting Principles Board continued to wrestle with this problem, but it was able only to agree, in *Opinion No. 31*, on a requirement that lease commitments be more fully disclosed in footnotes to the financial statements. This requirement did not, of course, affect the numbers in the financial statements themselves.

Until recently, proposals for reconciling the accounting for the use of leased assets with the accounting for the use of purchased assets have focused on making changes in the way *leased* assets are accounted for. The recognition of interest as a cost would lead to the opposite approach; it would change the method of accounting for *purchased* assets. In 1973, Philip Defliese, managing partner of Coopers & Lybrand and a past chairman of the Accounting Principles Board, developed a proposal along these lines. In addition to allowing for interest, he also would adjust the depreciation charge so that the sum of depreciation and interest (adjusted for income tax effects and, if appropriate, for major maintenance and renovation expenditures) would be approximately the same for each year of the asset's life. This total annual cost for the use of a purchased asset would closely correspond to the amount of annual payments that would be made for the same asset if it were leased. Since the annual interest cost decreases over time as the amount of capital tied up in the project becomes smaller, levelling of the annual cost requires that depreciaion be charged at increasing annual amounts. The annuity method of depreciation results in such a schedule of increasing charges.

Table 3-1
Comparative Income Statements
(millions of dollars)

	1971		1972		1973	
	As Reported	As Proposed	Reported	Proposed	Reported	Proposed
Sales	$339.4	$339.4	$370.5	$370.5	$453.9	$453.9
Cost of Sales	226.4	239.8	240.7	255.4	292.9	308.4
Other Expenses	89.5	91.9	95.6	98.4	116.2	119.7
Income Before Tax	$ 23.5	$ 7.7	$ 34.2	$ 16.7	$ 44.8	$ 25.8
Income Tax	8.8	8.8	16.5	16.5	21.9	21.9
Net Income (Loss)	$ 14.7	$ (1.1)	$ 17.7	$ 0.2	$ 22.9	$ 3.9

Defliese's proposal is carefully developed, with examples, in a paper submitted to the Securities and Exchange Commission.[2] It differs in some details with the procedure I describe in chapter 7, but the end result is basically the same, and I wholeheartedly support it.

Net Income and Shareholders' Equity

Table 3-1 shows how the proposal would affect the income statement. It was developed from data in an actual manufacturing company. The detailed procedures are described in chapter 7 and are not needed for our present purpose, which is to illustrate the effect of these procedures.

The most obvious difference between the statement as actually prepared and the way it would be prepared under the proposed procedure is the reduction in net income under the proposed procedure. This reduction arises because of the inclusion of equity interest as a cost. The message of the new income statement is that in 1971 the company did not earn quite enough to cover its equity interest cost, in 1972 it just about covered that cost, and in 1973 its earnings exceeded that cost by $3.9 million.

The change in the net income amount would take some getting used to, but once users of financial statements understood its significance, their knowledge of the company would be enhanced. The net income amount would essentially show how much management earned in excess of the minimum cost of equity capital. A company that did not generate enough revenue to cover all its costs, including the cost of the use of capital, would report a loss. A single such loss would not signify that a company was in any immediate danger of going bankrupt. If the loss persisted, however, it would mean that management was unable to use the capital entrusted to it in a way that covered its cost. If a company cannot earn enough on the average to pay for the cost of the capital that it uses, either a new management should be hired, or no new capital should be invested in the company.

Alternative Income Statement Format

The income statement in table 3-1 does not report what actually has happened to the shareholders' equity during the period. Defliese has proposed a way of doing this which, if I had thought of it, I would have included in that statement.[3] I present it separately here to insure that the credit for its development goes to him. It is illustrated in table 3-2, using data for 1973 for the same company shown in table 3-1, and with slight modification from his original format. This statement shows clearly what has happened to the shareholders' equity as a result of operations in 1973: it has increased by a total of $23.4 million, $19.5 million of which is equity interest cost and $3.9 million of which is profit above that cost.

Some other implications of the proposed reporting of income are described below.

Shift in Timing of Earnings

Under present practice, the total return to shareholders is reported as net income in the period in which revenue from sales of products is realized. Under the proposed plan, the shareholders' return would be divided into two elements, equity interest and profit. The equity interest portion would be added to retained earnings in the period in which the capital was employed, and only the profit portion would be reported in the period in which the product was sold. Thus, in years when production volume exceeded sales volume, the total shareholders' return would be larger under the proposed method than in the current method, because the equity interest cost on the additional inventory would be credited to retained earnings in that year. (Such a practice will not result in an overstatement of inventory values because the lower-of-cost-or-market rule would continue to apply.)

In general, credits to retained earnings (comprising the sum of equity interest and profit) would be made in an earlier time period under the proposed method than under the present method. In the case of the timber, for example, there would be a credit to retained earnings (and a corresponding debit to timber inventory) each year that the timber was maturing; it would represent the return on the equity capital that was employed in the

Table 3-2
Statement of Operations Proposed by Philip L. Defliese
(millions of dollars)[a]

Income Operations:		
Sales		$453.9
Less, Cost of sales	$308.4	
Other expenses	119.7	
Provision for income taxes	21.9	450.0
Profit from operations (after taxes)[b]		$ 3.9
(Per share of common stock: $1.30)		
Capital Operations:		
Imputed interest on net investment in facilities and operating assets (capitalized or charged to income operations)		$ 21.1
Less: Interest paid to creditors and lessors (after taxes)	$1.6	
Dividends on preferred stock	0	1.6
Net return on equity capital investment		19.5
(Per share of common stock $6.50)		
Total Income and Capital Operating Results		$ 23.4
Less: Dividends paid to common stock ($3.00 per share)		9.0
Current year's capital formed and retained		$ 14.4
Prior years' capital formed and retained (Bal. Jan. 1)		126.4
Total Capital Formed and Retained		$140.8

[a]Adapted, by permission of Philip I. Defliese.
[b]This is net operating income *after* all charges for holding costs of facilities, including interest on capital invested and depreciation.

timber inventory in that year. This is so, even though net income would be smaller under the proposed method, because equity interest has been excluded from net income.

Analysis of Company Performance

A company has not performed satisfactorily if it has not generated enough revenue to cover all its costs, including the cost of using capital. The current income statement does not show whether or not a company has met this fundamental test. It implies that any profit above the cost of debt interest is a "plus." Some analysts attempt to overcome this deficiency by making separate calculations that relate net income to the amount of equity capital. These calculations are necessarily crude, however, because the analyst cannot possibly allow for all the factors involving the use of capital that were described in chapter 2, and in particular for the effect of the timing differences described in the preceding section. In most cases, such adjustments are not even attempted. For example, the press in 1972 highlighted the fact that the Great Atlantic & Pacific Tea Company, once a highly profitable company, reported a loss. It should have started calling attention to A & P's problems as far back as 1968, for in that year the company earned less than its equity interest cost.

Comparisons of the net income of different companies is complicated by the different proportions of debt and equity capital in these companies. For two otherwise identical companies, whose operating performance was equally good, the one with the higher amount of debt capital will report lower net income. Again, analysts can make adjustments for this difference, but the proposed method eliminates the need for such adjustments. It gives a direct reading on how well the company has performed after covering all its capital costs.

Analysis of Stock Prices

In judging the attractiveness of a company's stock, the analyst, in addition to studying the company itself, must estimate whether or not the stock represents a good buy at its current market price. The price/earnings ratio is an important number in such an analysis. The number for earnings as presently calculated, however, is not well suited for inclusion in such a ratio. It consists of two essentially different components. First is the equity interest component, which fluctuates primarily with changes in the quantity of equity capital. If the cost of equity interest is 10 percent, the part of the market price that is associated with this component should be roughly ten times the equity interest cost per share. Second is the true profit component, which is highly volatile and difficult to forecast. If the interest and profit components were reported separately, analysts could focus their forecasting efforts on profit. They would be provided with a powerful analytical tool and undoubtedly would devise new rules of thumb, replacing the current "multiple," as aids in using this tool.

Analysts are not satisfied with current accounting numbers. They are well aware of the limitations of the reported balance sheet items. They know that the reported net income for a highly leveraged company must be interpreted differently from the net income of a company that has little debt, and they attempt to correct for these differences in an informal way. They should welcome an accounting system that makes some of these corrections explicitly.

Closely Held Companies

The advantages discussed here apply to publicly owned companies. There is no thought of depriving persons who own their own companies from the pleasure of measuring profits according to the proprietary concept. They can work long hours at no recorded salary cost, and they can invest their own capital at no recorded interest cost. The "profit" reported in accordance with such practices will be higher than the true profit because of the omission of these costs. This profit figure is nevertheless a source of gratification to the owner.

Objections to the Proposal

Basic Objection

Although most informed persons grant the theoretical validity of the argument that interest is an element of cost, many argue that the explicit recognition of this cost will cause more confusion than benefit. A change in accounting is proposed that will result in substantially different meanings for certain asset amounts on the balance sheet and in a fundamentally different meaning for the net income item on the income statement. At the time when the change is made, readers of financial statements will not understand either the nature or the significance of the new numbers. In particular, the meanings of earnings per share, the price/earnings ratio, times interest earned, and other ratios will be altered. Such measures must be expressed differently than they now are if they are to have any meaning at all. New overall indicators of performance will have to be developed. Analysts judge financial statements on the basis of their personal norms of good or bad performance. They have gradually developed these norms from their study of many financial statements. They must now create a new set of norms based on the new principle of accounting. It is argued that the business community should not be subjected to this painful process of adjustment unless there are compelling reasons for doing so.

This argument continues by asserting that the reasons for making the change are not compelling. Essentially, it is said, the proposal is that the amount now designed as net income be divided into two parts—an interest element and a profit element—and although the profit element is shown seaprately on the income statement, the two parts are combined in the retained earnings account, just as they are in current accounting. It is further said that this does little more than record explicitly something that informed readers of financial statements already know and take into account in their analysis. The return on investment ratio that is now commonly calculated tells approximately the same story that would be told by the recording of equity interest, it is argued. At present, a company is judged in part by whether its return on investment is satisfactory. A corresponding judgment will be made under the proposed method, and although the numbers will be different, the final judgment, the argument runs, will not be substantially affected; that is, a company whose performance is judged to be satisfactory according to its financial statements as currently constructed will also be judged to have satisfactory performance under the proposed accounting method.

In any event, the critics say, the failure to recognize interest as an element of cost is only one of several ways in which accounting does not correspond to principles of economics. Accounting does not record assets at realizable values, let alone at the present value of their future earnings; accounting does not recognize holding gains; accounting does not adjust for changes in the price level; and so on. Why focus on this one discrepancy between accounting and economic reality, and disregard the others? Unless all of them are taken into account, it is said, the financial statements will not actually report the true facts. Indeed, there is the danger that readers will be misled into believing that with this one adjustment the financial statements will then reflect the true facts.

Discussion of the Basic Objection

The argument stated above has three parts: (1) there will be great confusion and misunderstanding during a transition period; (2) judgments based on the new way of reporting accounting events will not be significantly different than those made now; and (3) the proposal deals with only one of several inadequacies of accounting. Of these, I regard the first as a much more important argument than the other two.

There will indeed be a transition period of much confusion, and the headaches of this period will be worthwhile only if the long-run gains are substantial. But the person who made this argument to me most cogently went on to say: "This may in itself not be a better basis of objection than to insist that because we are used to it we must continue to live with yards, feet and inches rather than adopting a metric system." Any significant change involves a transition period; the period of confusion is often shorter than people predict. The British easily made the change to a decimal currency system. If the long-term gains are substantial, the headaches caused by the transition period are worthwhile.

The argument that the proposal does no more than record explicitly a fact that users of financial statements now allow for implicitly, is, I believe, not strong. At most, the argument refers to the interpretation of net income. There are few circumstances in which analysts have the information required to adjust asset amounts for the effect of interest and even fewer in which they attempt to make such adjustments. In interpreting net income, a return on investment calculation may tell roughly the same story as that told by recording interest in the accounts, but then again it may not. Return on investment does not reflect the differences in timing that were described earlier in this chapter, and these differences can be important. At best, the correspondence is rough, and the story told under the proposed method is demonstrably more realistic.

The argument that the proposal does not cure all the ills of accounting is, I believe, also weak. Accounting is an evolving discipline. In recent years progress has been quite rapid. But progress is made one step at a time. The change advocated here is one such step, and there will of course be others. Accounting will never correspond exactly to economic realities; it is not feasible to do so, and users of accounting information must understand its limitations. If users believe that accounting says more than it actually can say, the solution is education, not abandonment of attempts to do the best job that can be done.

Some say that accounting is already too complicated, and that accountants should move in the direction of simplicity, rather than adding further complications. Carried to its extreme, this argument would reduce accounting to a system of measuring only cash receipts and disbursements, for the complications of accounting arise principally from efforts to measure the flow of resources and the amounts of assets and equities on other than a cash basis. A business is a complicated organism; the objective of accounting should be to aid in understanding it as fully as possible. Simplicity, at the expense of a loss in comprehension, is no virtue.

Removal of Legal Distinctions

Critics of the proposal also maintain that its implementation would combine two quite different kinds of capital: debt capital, which, together with its interest, is a legal claim against assets, and equity capital, which has only a residual claim. This argument is not true with respect to the balance sheet, and it is not relevant with respect to the income statement. The proposal has no effect on the practice of distinguishing on the balance sheet between liabilities and shareholders' equity nor on the practice of reporting separately on each significant item within the liabilities and shareholders' equity categories. On the income statement, the inclusion of interest on equity capital as a cost seems to me to be no different than the inclusion of depreciation. Neither of these items is a "legal claim"; neither necessarily corresponds to the cash flow in the period.

Shareholders' equity would not be significantly affected by the proposal, because one or more accounts in the shareholders' equity section would be credited both for the amount of reported profit and for the interest on equity capital; the sum of these is similar (except for timing differences) to the amount of net income that is credited to retained earnings under current practice. The shareholders' equity accounts can therefore continue to perform their traditional role as a legal limitation on the amount of dividends that can be declared. In any event, it is unusual today for the decision on dividends to be affected by the amount of retained earnings. The situation arises primarily when dividend payments are restricted by bond covenants. Since retained earnings in the proposed method will differ somewhat from retained earnings as currently reported, these covenants will need to be reexamined, but it seems likely that changes will not be required in most cases.

On the income statement, no principle of accounting requires that cash costs be separated from accrued costs; nor is there a principle that gives a higher status to one type of cost as compared with another. Deferred income tax, which is not a cash cost, and which indeed may never become a cash cost, is a legitimate income statement item. An even closer case in point is bond interest expense, which, when bonds are sold at other than par, is the algebraic sum of the cash interest cost and the amortized portion of the discount or premium; the latter is a noncash cost.

Behind this argument lurks the lingering belief that equity interest is not really a cost at all. In the same way, managers some years ago believed that an addition to retained earnings was a costless way of raising capital.

Conservatism

When equity interest is included as one element of product cost, and when such products remain in inventory at the end of an accounting period, a shareholders' equity account is credited for such amounts in an earlier time period than would be the case under current practice. For example, if product inventory at the end of 1974 includes, as an element of cost, $10 of equity interest as a cost for the use of capital in the manufacturing process in 1974, there would also be a corresponding credit of $10 to retained earnings or some similar new account under the proposed method. Under the current method, by contrast, activities relating to the manufacture of products have no effect on retained earnings until the period in which the products are sold. Under current practice, therefore, the $10 would not be added to retained earnings until 1975. Any accounting practice that has the effect of adding something to retained earnings in an earlier period than would be the case with an alternative practice is said to be not conservative. More specifically, it is said that unless the products in question are produced to customer order, there is no assurance that they ever will be sold; or, if sold, that the price will be high enough to recover all costs, including interest. Consequently, the recognition of equity interest is alleged to result in recognizing profits before they are earned.

If "profit" is defined as accounting currently defines it, as including both interest on equity capital as well as what the economist calls profit, then this criticism is warranted. If, however, one accepts the view that a business has not earned a profit until its revenues exceed all of its costs, including interest on total capital, then the proposed practice does not in fact record profits earlier than they were earned; it only records costs as they were incurred. This shift in the concept of profit may be difficult to get used to, but this does not per se make the new concept undesirable. Stated another way, profit as currently measured by the accountant involves both the recognition of revenues and the recognition of cost expiration. If the cost of using capital attaches to goods in inventory and is thus postponed to be matched against future revenue, this does not make the measurement of profit "less conservative"; rather, it is simply an application of the concept that costs should be matched with revenue.

It is a basic concept of financial accounting that revenue should not be recognized until it has been realized, but the proposal does not affect that concept. It has nothing to do with revenue; it affects only costs. (Indeed, the proposal does not appear to conflict with any of the concepts of accounting as listed in such authoritative sources as *Statement No. 4* of the Accounting Principles Board.[4])

As a practical matter, the danger does exist that some companies will subvert the proposed principle in an attempt to increase reported earnings, just as some land development and franchise companies have subverted the realization principle for the same purpose. The greatest danger is in the case of self-constructed plant, because the effect of the proposal is to report equity interest during the period of construction, rather than a corresponding amount over the life of the plant, as is the current practice, and the resultant difference in timing of earnings can be substantial. For several reasons, I think these dangers may be exaggerated.

First, the amount of interest and its application to specific assets will be objectively determined, by procedures described in chapters 6 and 7. Differences of opinion, such as those involved in the recognition of franchise revenue, or in the circumstances in which a sales contract for land should be recognized, or in whether research and development efforts will produce adequate future income, are not involved.

Second, in the case of plant, no business would undertake construction unless it had sound economic reasons for doing so. Interest, although an element of cost, is only a minor part of the total plant project. Thus, it is highly unlikely that plant would be constructed simply to generate a credit to shareholders' equity.

Third, the lower-of-cost-or-market rule continues in full force and protects against the unwarranted inflation of inventory amounts. In the ordinary situation, inventory amounts that include interest will still be lower than the net realizable value of the inventory; in those few situations in which this is not the case, the cost-or-market principle requires that an appropriate writedown be made.

Omission of Interest

Some people, although impressed with the fact that accounting records debt interest but not equity interest, suggest that the solution is to omit both types of interest from the accounts. If this were done, the final item on the income statement would be "net income after taxes but before interest," and a separate statement would report how this amount was divided between the two sources of capital, debt and equity. Such an approach is consistent with the entity concept, which requires that similar treatment be given to the two sources of capital.

Insofar as the income statement alone is concerned, this approach does have an advantage over present practice. This is, however, its only advantage. Since no recognition would be given to the cost of capital employed for cost objectives, none of the other benefits could be achieved.

Other Criticisms

The proposal is also criticized on the grounds that there is no feasible way of determining the cost of equity interest. Discussion of this point is deferred to chapter 6.

Welsch and Davidson have collected from the literature some twenty-four arguments against the proposal advanced here.[5] At one stage, I considered discussing them one by one, but I have decided not to subject the reader to this amount of detail. Most of these arguments, including all the important ones, have been addressed in the preceding paragraphs. The remainder deal with semantics or are based on misconceptions about the nature of accounting information.

Summary

The recognition of interest as a cost would increase the amounts reported on the balance sheet for manufactured inventory, for inventory held a long period of time, and for plant and equipment that is either self-constructed or paid for in advance of receipt. The increase would be particularly significant for timber, petroleum and other mineral reserves, and for inventories of goods that must be aged. The proposal to charge interest, coupled with the annuity method of depreciation, would make the annual cost of using owned productive assets comparable with the cost of using leased assets.

Net income would be smaller, reflecting the recognition of equity interest as an element of cost rather than as a component of income. The increase in shareholders' equity in a period would not necessarily be smaller than it is under current practice, however, for shareholders' equity would be increased by the sum of net income and equity interest. The net impact on shareholders' equity would depend on timing differences, that is, on whether the amount of equity interest that is included in the asset accounts increased or decreased during the period.

These changes would result in an income statement that gives a picture of a company's performance that is more in line with the economic realities, and that is more comparable with the income statement of other companies that use different proportions of debt and equity capital.

Critics of the proposal are correct in arguing that these changes would require a considerable period of adjustment before their significance was thoroughly understood, but this price must be paid for any significant change. Critics are not correct in asserting that the proposal would blur the legal distinction between debt capital and equity capital. The proposal does not violate the doctrine of conservatism; although there is some possibility of abuse, these are minimal because the proposal allows little room for subjective opinions, because it would not lead to uneconomic decisions, and because inventory amounts would continue to be subject to the lower-of-cost-or-market rule.

4

Implications for Public Policy

Many government agencies use accounting information obtained from business firms. The inclusion of interest as an element of cost would facilitate the work of these agencies. It would also help to correct erroneous impressions about business that tend to become translated into public policy.

Setting of Rates

For many years, regulatory bodies have set rates that were intended to provide companies with a fair return on the capital they employed. They do this in a roundabout way, however. In some calculations, interest on debt capital is included as an explicit element of cost, and the fair return on equity capital is included as a separate item, arrived at by formulas that the agencies have created and that the courts have approved. In other calculations, interest is excluded as an element of cost, and a return on total capital is calculated. The accounting treatment of interest on a self-constructed plant which, as noted above, is allowed as an element of cost, is complicated and sometimes controversial. The whole process of rate setting would be simpler and more straightforward if regulatory agencies adopted the principle that interest on both debt and equity capital should be explicitly included in rate calculations as an element of cost.

Price Control

In November 1972, the newly appointed Federal Price Commission tackled the problem of finding a way to specify the maximum selling prices that all companies could charge. Although the commission recognized the conceptual soundness of the principle that prices should provide a fair return on capital employed, it rapidly concluded that there was no way of making such an approach operational. The accounting records of American companies were inadequate to permit the calculation of the capital cost that was an element of such a price. The commission did use the capital-employed concept in a few exceptional situations, but for the thousands of companies from which regular reports were required, an alternative approach had to be developed. Rules were formulated that required a company to set selling

47

prices in such a way that its current margins on individual products were not increased and that the resulting profit margin percentage for the company as a whole did not exceed the average profit margin percentage for the best two out of the three preceding years.

These rules were inequitable, and the commission knew that they were inequitable. Table 4-1 (derived from the commission's own analysis of published data) illustrates the inequity. The exhibit tells a rather shocking story. It shows that the rules had the effect of permitting 12 percent of the companies to earn a pretax return on total capital of 30 percent or more, but at the same time they prohibited 20 percent of the companies from earning as much as a 10 percent pretax return. Relief for a few of these low-profit companies was provided by making an exception to the general rules on a case-by-case basis. No action was taken to inhibit price increases by the high-profit companies, however, and these companies did not, of course, inform the Price Commission of their high return on capital employed. Essentially, the same rules were continued in Phase IV of the price control program, as instituted in 1973 by the Cost of Living Council.

Given the existing accounting systems used by American business, there is no way to devise a system that would avoid such inequities. An equitable solution would be possible if debt and equity interest were included routinely as an element of cost in the accounting systems of American companies. Under these circumstances, the rule could have been that prices should be calculated so as to recover all costs, including interest cost, plus a profit margin. With such a rule no company would have been denied the opportunity to set prices that were high enough to recover the costs of the capital that it employed. At the other end of the scale, companies would be inhibited from increasing their prices to the point where they earned an unjustifiably high return on capital employed.

Contract Pricing

Inclusion of interest as an element of cost would lead to a better basis of pricing cost-type contracts. Many tens of billions of dollars of payments by the government to private companies are based on such contracts. Although the situation is similar in most government agencies, I shall discuss the application of the proposal to contracts let by the Department of Defense, both because the amount of money involved in cost-type defense contracts is far larger than that in any other agency and also because I am more familiar with the situation in Defense.

For many years, the price of cost-type contracts has been arrived at by using a profit margin that was essentially a percentage of cost. (The price cannot legally be stated as cost plus a percentage of cost, so the profit is

Table 4-1
Estimated Effect of Price Commission Policies

Allowed pretax return on capital	Companies permitted to earn such returns	
	Number	Percent
30% or over	168	11.6
20% to 30%	341	23.1
10% to 20%	664	45.4
Less than 10%	292	19.9
Total	1,465	100.0

Source: Computed by Price Commission staff from *COMPUSTAT* Data.

actually stated as a dollar amount; however, the dollar amount is found by taking a percentage of estimated cost. In some cases an adjustment is made to take account of the difference between estimated costs and actual costs.) This practice is basically inequitable. It results in high profits to contractors with a high turnover of capital, and yields inadequate profits to contractors with a low capital turnover. (The pricing guidelines of the Department of Defense do provide for special treatment of contractors that do not use much of their own capital. This "source of resources" adjustment subtracts either one or two percentage points from the profit margin. In practice, this adjustment has been used only rarely.)

Table 4-2 illustrates this point. It shows how the return on capital employed would differ for two companies, producing identical end products, and which are identical in all respects except that Company A owns its plant and equipment and Company B leases its plant and equipment. In each case, the contract price is calculated at 107 percent of cost. Company A employs $1,000,000 of capital, and its capital turnover is approximately one (=$963,000 ÷ $1,000,000). Its $63,000 profit is a return on capital of only 6.3 percent. Company B, which owns no plant and equipment, employs only $200,000 of capital, and its capital turnover is almost five times (= $974,000 ÷ $200,000). Its plant and equipment costs, in the form of lease payments, are higher than the corresponding depreciation expense for Company A because the lease payments include compensation for the capital employed by the lessor.

Since Company B's costs are higher than Company A's, and since the profit margin is calculated as a percentage of cost, the government pays a higher price to Company B than to Company A. Because of its high capital turnover, Company B's profit of $64,000 gives it a 32 percent return on its capital employed. Even if the government discovers and disallows the extra $10,000 of lease payment costs, which it has attempted to do in recent

Table 4-2
Relation of Capital Turnover and Return on Capital

Cost elements	*000 omitted*	
	Company A	*Company* B
Costs other than for plant and equipment	$ 800	$800
Depreciation	100	0
Lease costs	0	110
Total costs	$ 900	$910
Profit margin, 7 percent	63	64
Contract price	$ 963	$974
Capital employed		
Working capital	$ 200	$200
Plant and equipment	800	0
Total capital employed	$1000	$200
Return on capital		
$63 ÷ $1,000	6.3 percent	
$64 ÷ $200		32 percent

years, Company B would nevertheless earn a return of 26 percent on its capital employed, compared to the 6.3 percent earned by Company A.

In addition to leasing, contractors can increase their capital turnover by subcontracting component manufacture, by insisting on rapid progress payments, and even by failing to install cost-cutting equipment.

That the example given in table 4-2 is not an extreme or isolated situation is shown in table 4-3, which summarizes a 1971 study of profits on defense contracts made by the US General Accounting Office (GAO). Some contracts earned extremely high returns on capital employed, whereas 12 percent were performed at a loss. Although in part this dispersion is accounted for by other factors, an important cause of difference is the variation in capital turnover. The GAO study concluded that, for the companies studied, although the average return on sales for their defense business was only half that of their commercial business, the average return on capital for defense business was almost the same as that of their commercial business. This is because the capital turnover for defense business was typically much higher than that for commercial business. The GAO recommended that in negotiating the profit margin on contracts, the government should emphasize the amount of capital employed.

As another indication, Senator William Proxmire reported that of 131

Table 4-3

GAO Study of Defense Contractors: Variation in Return on Capital Employed, 146 Contracts

	Percent of Total Contracts
Loss	12
Return of:	
0.1 to 20%	32
20.1 to 40%	29
40.1 to 60%	13
60.1 to 80%	6
80.1 to 100%	3
Over 100%	5
Total	100

Source: Comptroller General, *General Industry Profit Study* (March 17, 1971), pp. 19, 20.

defense firms who in 1972 were required by the Renegotiation Board to refund excess profits, 64 firms had profits of 35 percent or more on capital employed, even after the deduction of these refunds.[1]

The percentage-of-cost approach motivates the contractor to make unsound decisions: to lease assets, even though the net cost of owned assets may be less; to refrain from introducing cost-saving equipment; to seek maximum progress payments for himself, but to delay payments to his subcontractors; to maintain inadequate inventory levels for material not subject to progress payment, and in general to reduce the amount of his own capital employed on the contract to the lowest possible level. These practices increase the final price paid for the item.

In the United Kingdom, the Federal Republic of Germany, and in other European countries, the defects in percentage-of-cost pricing were recognized earlier, and in these countries defense-contract pricing shifted several years ago to a return-on-capital approach.

After much debate and many studies, in 1973 the Department of Defense began to use an approach that took into account the amount of capital employed.[2] Since contractors' accounting systems did not record the cost of using capital, the new method had to arrive at a comparable result by a complicated, roundabout formula. A more rational and direct approach to pricing cost-type defense contracts would include interest on capital employed as an allowable cost.[3] The fee, or profit allowance, would be correspondingly smaller and would be a reward for good management and a good organization. An interest charge would provide a more exact way to measure the appropriate reward for the capital used than is possible by including an estimate of return on capital employed as part of the profit margin. It would permit the development of incentive devices that would encourage "capital saving" actions similar to the incentives that are now used to encourage cost savings. (Although not relevant for purposes of the present discussion, I mention that the profit margin should not be related *solely* to capital employed. In part, profit should be related to the amount of human resources employed.)

Furthermore, if interest were counted as a cost, a peculiarity in the present government contracting practice with respect to nonprofit organizations would be removed. If a university or other nonprofit organization uses its own capital on a contract, it should be compensated for that use. That is, if it ties up endowment funds in a new building or equipment used for government work, it should be compensated for the loss of the income that would have been earned had these funds been invested in income-producing securities. Under the current rubric, however, compensation for the use of capital is called profit. The inclusion in a contract of a provision for such compensation, therefore, creates the phenomenon of a nonprofit organization earning a profit. Contracting officers are reluctant to include such an allowance. If the same amount were labeled "interest," which it is, this peculiarity would disappear.

Public Attitude

If equity interest becomes an element of cost, the fact that a correspondingly smaller amount of profit will be reported can have highly desirable social consequences. The general public tends to think of profit as it is presently defined as an amount that is not actually needed in a business, or in any event as an amount that could be reduced with few serious consequences. It is difficult to convince people that a business must earn enough to cover the cost of its capital if it is to survive. If revenue is not at least large enough to recover the total interest cost, capital will flow out of the business, the company will shrink in size, and jobs will be lost. This message would be transmitted to the public more clearly if the cost of using capital were labeled accurately—as a cost.

Schreiber points out, for example, that in the Federal Republic of Germany, true profits (after deduction of interest) in good years actually amount to 8.5 percent of national income, which is such a small fraction of the total that prices would not be substantially reduced even if profits were reduced by a considerable percentage.[4] Another example: A friend told me that he heard a local politician state that it was ridiculous to permit the New England Telephone Company to earn an 8 percent profit at the same time that he could only earn 5 percent at a savings bank.

Effect on Profit Margin Ratios

Net income is frequently related to sales revenue. The consumer wonders why some companies take 5 percent of their payment as profit, while other companies take only 1 percent. One important reason for these differences in profit ratios is, of course, the difference in the amount of capital employed. A department store that turns its capital only twice a year needs a 5 percent profit on sales to earn a 10 percent return on its capital; whereas a supermarket that turns its capital ten times a year can earn a 10 percent return on its capital with a profit on sales of only 1 percent. The public does not appreciate these relationships. The facts would be clearer if interest were counted as an element of cost. The department store would report a heavy interest cost per dollar of sales and the supermarket a low interest cost, and their profit, after interest, would be brought closer together.

Misconceptions About Interest

The rational discussion of many problems is impeded by misunderstanding of the nature of interest. Arguments about the allowability of interest in cost-type defense contracts illustrate this point. As demonstrated above, the best way of arriving at a fair profit on defense contracts is to take account of capital employed. The next best way is to relate profits to costs, excluding all interest; this is current practice. The *worst* way of pricing is to allow interest on *debt* capital as an element of cost and to disregard interest on equity capital. This would reward companies that have a high proportion of debt and, indeed, would encourage companies to have a higher proportion of debt than is prudent. It makes no economic sense at all. Nevertheless, in the discussions over the last ten years of contract pricing methods—within the Department of Defense, between defense officials and representatives of industry, and in congressional hearings—the argument invariably is made that interest on *debt* capital should be allowed as an element of cost. Although such a position cannot be justified economically, there is a justification for it in accounting: debt interest is recorded, whereas equity interest is not. The recognition of equity interest as an element of cost in financial accounting would end these protracted, fallacious, and fruitless arguments.

This misconception persists. For example, an article in the February 1973 issue of *Management Accounting* recommends a number of changes in the Armed Services Procurement Regulations. The article states: "By all normal and reasonable standards, interest should be allowable."[5] By "interest," the author means debt interest. He is dead wrong.

In general, the impression is widespread that interest on debt capital is a cost (but not a cost that is properly part of product cost), and that interest on equity capital is not really a cost at all. Underlying this misconception is the feeling that if interest were really a cost element, like labor and material, accountants would record it as such. If accountants do record interest, this misconception would disappear, and public discussion could focus on relevant matters.

Income Taxes

For tax purposes, interest on debt capital has always been allowed as a deduction despite some opposition, such as the comment by Representative Hickman of Pennsylvania during debate on the Income Tax Act of 1862:

If a man chooses to go in debt to the amount of half the value of his farm, that is a matter of propriety for him to consider; but it is not a matter which should induce the Government to relieve him from taxation.[6]

Hickman's argument against the inclusion of debt interest did not gain support. Subsequently, in the tax acts of 1864, 1870, 1894, 1909, 1913, and down to the present, the deduction of debt interest has been permitted. No deduction has been allowed for dividends or any other item associated with the cost of equity capital. Similarly, in English law, since at least 1799 (39 Geo. 3, c. 13), interest actually paid could be deducted, but interest on equity capital was specifically not allowed as a deduction.

The tax distinction between debt interest, which is deductible, and equity interest, which is not, has some undesirable consequences. Companies devise instruments close enough to being debt so that their interest payments qualify as a tax deduction but which have as few as possible of the constraints associated with normal debt. More important, since the real cost of debt is only about half its stated pretax interest cost, whereas the real cost of equity is 100 percent of its pretax cost, some companies are tempted to assume a greater burden of debt than is prudent.

Dividends are taxed twice, once at the corporate level, since they correspond to a part of taxable income, and again when they are received by the shareholder. Debt interest is taxed only to the person who receives it. Added to this, capital gains are taxed at a rate only about half that at which dividends are taxed; these are strong reasons why companies should pay only nominal cash dividends. Dividends no longer correspond roughly to equity interest, which was typically the case some years ago.

In only a few situations should taxable income logically differ from accounting income: (1) tax provisions designed to stimulate the economy, such as the investment credit, or intended to further other public policies; (2) situations in which accounting principles permit more latitude than is prudent for effective tax administration, as is the case with the nondeductibility for tax purposes of most estimates of future losses; and (3) for tax purposes, income should not be recorded prior to the period in which cash is available to pay the tax on this income. With exceptions such as these, corporate tax regulations and accounting principles are both designed to measure the same phenomena, and there is no logical reason why they should differ. None of these reasons applies to the proposal discussed here.

Conceptually, therefore, it would be a good idea to remove the discrepancy between the definition of taxable income and the proposed definition of accounting income by allowing interest on equity capital as a deductible expense for income tax purposes. This would require some corresponding change to make up the lost tax revenue. However desirable such a move may be in concept, great practical difficulties obstruct its achievement in the near future, and it is not a part of the present proposal. (In October 1974, President Ford proposed that certain preferred dividends be made deductible, which is a step in the right direction.) The fact that the gap between taxable income and accounting income would be widened if the proposal were adopted for financial accounting purposes, but not for tax purposes, is not important. Business can cope with this discrepancy just as it copes with a fairly long list of other differences between taxable income and accounting income.[7]

5 Implications for Management Accounting

As noted in chapter 2, many companies already incorporate interest cost in accounting information that is developed as an aid to management, and this is an important reason for believing that the inclusion of interest as a cost would be useful in financial reporting. Furthermore, there is no inherent reason why management accounting information must be consistent with financial accounting. Nevertheless, the recognition of interest as a cost in financial accounting would have significant consequences for the accounting information used in managing a business, and some of these are discussed in this chapter.

Benefits of Harmonization

Although no law or principle requires it, consistency between financial accounting and management accounting is desirable for two good reasons: consistency saves work, and consistency has psychological advantages.

Advantage of Saving Work

A company has no choice but to collect information adequate for financial reporting purposes; such information must be reported in accordance with generally accepted financial accounting principles. If this information is not adequate or appropriate for management's needs, a special system for collecting management information must be created. The effort required to operate such a separate system, however, is often judged to be greater than the value of its results. Thus, to the extent that the management accounting and financial accounting systems are harmonized, the work involved in operating two systems is reduced, and some practices will be adopted which, although desirable, are judged to be not worth the effort of operating a separate system.

For example, the inclusion of interest as an element of cost would greatly facilitate a rational system for recording the transfer of products and services from one profit center to another in situations where transfer prices cannot be based on market prices. In such situations, a transfer price

57

that included interest would credit the selling profit center with a return on its capital employed. Some companies do use such a transfer price system, but they must go to the trouble of removing the interest components from cost for purposes of financial reporting. If the internal flow of goods and services is at all complicated, and particularly if the amount of capital employed varies widely from one profit center to another, the task of purging the interest component from the final product cost is so complicated that few companies are willing to undertake it. These companies therefore make transfers at an amount that excludes interest, or they add a crude allowance for profit that does not come close to the real cost of capital employed.

Under these circumstances, profit-center performance reports can give grossly inaccurate information about the real performance of various divisions. In the extreme, if a profit center is credited only with the cost, in the conventional sense, of the product it transfers to another profit center, the selling profit center appears not to be earning any return at all on the capital that it uses. If interest were counted as an element of cost in a cost-based transfer pricing system, transfer pricing practices would be simplified. In many situations, the amounts used for internal transfers would be incorporated, unchanged, in inventory and cost-of-sales on the financial statements.

Psychological Advantages

Harmonizing financial accounting and management accounting has important psychological benefits as well. There is a widespread belief that financial accounting numbers are "real" and that numbers constructed according to other principles are "soft" or even "phony." The contrast between debt interest and equity interest provides an excellent example of this. Debt interest is thought to be a real cost, as proved by its appearance in the financial accounts, but many people do not believe that equity interest is a real cost, despite what the economics books say and despite the fact that when they think about it they realize that equity capital is not obtained for nothing. They reason that if equity interest were a real cost, accountants would treat it as such.

An example of how this misconception impedes a rational discussion of pricing policy in defense contracts was given in chapter 4. The same type of problem arises with a company. Many companies measure divisional profitability by what is loosely called return on investment (ROI), but there are so many versions of the ROI calculation that a person not thoroughly familiar with the system used by a particular company often cannot understand what profitability reports mean. Is the return calculated before debt interest? If so, has an adjustment been made for the tax effect of debt interest? Does the investment include all assets? or only all tangible assets? or all producing assets? Since the ROI calculation is not part of generally accepted accounting principles, there is no uniformity in the way various companies answer these questions.

Accounting for Capital Acquisitions

Current financial accounting principles also lead to another type of distortion, which pertains to the treatment of newly acquired assets. A capital acquisition can have the effect of decreasing reported profits in the early years of its life, even though it is in fact a profitable investment. This happens because the resulting depreciation charge is calculated on a straight-line, or even accelerated, basis for financial accounting purposes, whereas the profitability calculation that is made when proposed capital acquisitions are being analyzed implicitly assumes a much smaller amount of depreciation in the early years. In these circumstances, management may reject a proposed capital acquisition simply because of its depressing effect on near-term profits as reported in the accounts, although it is economically justifiable over its whole life. If interest were counted as a cost and if a corresponding change were made in the depreciation schedule so that the sum of interest and depreciation in each year of an asset's life were constant, accounting numbers would more closely parallel the calculations made in analyzing proposed capital acquisitions.

The relationships involved are fundamentally the same as the relationships between purchased assets and leased assets as discussed in chapter 3. To understand what they are, one needs to consider the economic realities associated with analyses of proposed capital acquisitions and the difference between the usual accounting measurement of return on investment and the concept used by the analyst. The meaning of return on investment used by the analyst is illustrated by the numbers in table 5-1. This exhibit demonstrates that a proposed investment in a machine costing $1000, which is estimated to generate a cash inflow of $250 per year for five years, is expected to earn 8 percent on the amount at risk each year.

The analyst does not actually make the year-by-year calculation shown in table 5-1. He uses a calculator or table that shows him directly that the return is 8 percent. The exhibit merely demonstrates the precise meaning of return on investment: that the $250 annual earnings will, over the five-year period, both recoup the investment of $1000 and also yield a return of 8 percent on the amount of the investment that has not yet been recouped at the end of any year. For example, in the first year the whole $1000 is outstanding; 8 percent of this, or $80, is "set aside" as return, and the

Table 5-1
Analysis of Investment

Year	Cash inflow (A)	Return at 8 percent of investment outstanding (B)	Balance: capital recovery (C)=(A − B)	Investment outstanding end of year (D)
0	$	$	$	$1,000
1	250	80	170	830
2	250	66	184	646
3	250	52	198	448
4	250	36	214	234
5	250	16	234	0

remainder of the $250, or $170, goes to reduce the investment, making it $830. In the second year, the return is 8 percent of $830, or $66, and so on.

In the situation illustrated above, the return *is* 8 percent in the sense that (if things work out as expected) the company recoups the amount of capital it has risked and in addition receives 8 percent each year on the funds still at risk that year. This meaning of return on investment is universally accepted in capital-budgeting analysis.

If the machine is actually acquired, however, and if the cash inflows are, in fact, $250 per year for five years, the usual accounting records will not show a return of 8 percent either in any single year or in an "average" year. For example, under the straight-line method of depreciation, the accounting records would show the results illustrated in table 5-2.

The computed return on gross assets makes no allowance for the fact that part of the initial investment is being recovered each year, and this calculation, therefore, understates the true return. The computed return on net assets does, through the depreciation mechanism, allow for the recovery of the initial investment, but the pattern of recovery implied by the straight-line method of depreciation is not the same as the pattern of recovery implicit in the concept of return on investment, which is that shown in the capital recovery column of table 5-1. Use of an accelerated depreciation method (such as double declining balance or sum-of-the-years' digits) makes the discrepancy even greater, because the pattern of the accelerated methods is the opposite of that in column C, which shows increasing amounts of recovery each year.[1]

Accounting reports would reflect the economic flows—that is, they would match the numbers in table 5-1—if the following two principles were followed:

Table 5-2
Conventional Accounting Results

Year	Gross assets	Average[a] net assets	Net income[b]	Return Computed on gross	Return on net
1	$1000	$900	$50	5%	5.5%
2	1000	700	50	5	7.1
3	1000	500	50	5	10.0
4	1000	300	50	5	16.7
5	1000	100	50	5	50.0

[a]Average of beginning and ending book values.
[b]Cash earnings, $250, minus depreciation, $200. Income taxes are disregarded.

1. Use a method of depreciation that matches the implicit recovery of the investment.
2. Charge interest for the use of capital as an element of cost.

The annuity method of depreciation matches the investment recovery for investments in which the annual cash inflows are level; that is, the annual amounts credited to accumulated depreciation and debited to depreciation expense in the annuity method are the same as those in column C in table 5-1. If this method of depreciation were used, the reported net income of each year would be 8 percent of the net asset value at the beginning of that year. This change, taken by itself, would therefore make the financial statements reconcilable with the analyst's concept of return on investment. The annuity method of depreciation was more common fifty years ago than now, although it is still used by some utilities. It is permitted by generally accepted accounting principles, which state that any "systematic and rational" method of distributing net asset cost over useful life is acceptable.

With respect to the second rule, the capital charge would be the interest cost of capital employed, as proposed in this book. The capital employed is the book value of the asset in the given year. In the situation described above, if the interest cost is 8 percent and if cash inflows actually were $250 each year, the reported net income would be zero. For example, in Year 3, the income statement (disregarding all items other than those relevant to this investment) would be:

Revenue		$250
Depreciation	$198	
Interest	52	250
Net income		0

An income statement constructed in accordance with these rules, and for an investment estimated to earn exactly the interest rate, would show zero net income for each year that the actual situation came out exactly as estimated, and would show positive or negative net income for years in which the estimates were exceeded or not realized, respectively. Moreover, projects that were accepted because it was anticipated that they would earn more than their interest cost would increase net income to the extent that these expectations were realized.

It can be argued that the manager should not be influenced by the misleading results in conventional accounting reports: if a proposed capital acquisition is economically justified, it should be made, even if its effect is to decrease reported profits in the early years, and readers of reports should make a mental adjustment for the aberration. This, I believe, is asking human beings to behave in a quite abnormal way. The simple solution is to record interest as an element of cost.

Inventory Management

In deciding how much of a given item to order, an inventory manager is supposed to strike an optimum balance between the high inventory carrying costs that result when a few large orders are placed in a given time period, on the one hand, and the high ordering costs (or setup costs) that result when many small orders are placed, on the other hand. The manager may use an Economic Order Quantity equation as a basis for the decision, or he may make a judgmental decision. The equation recognizes explicitly the interest cost associated with carrying inventory, and a judgmental decision should recognize implicitly that the capital tied up in inventory does have a cost.

If interest cost is not recognized explicitly in the accounting system, however, a conflict is created between the message conveyed by the EOQ equation and the message conveyed by the accounting system. The accounting system fully recognizes the ordering costs, which are essentially cash costs, but it understates the carrying costs by the omission of interest. Thus, the accounting system suggests that the amount ordered should be larger than the optimum amount.[2]

This lack of congruence between the accounting system and the equation can be corrected by including interest as an element of cost in the accounting system.

Divisional Performance Measurement

In measuring the profitability of a division or other profit center, an increasing number of companies are finding it useful to take account of the capital employed in the division. If adequate attention is not focused on the management of assets, division managers tend to accumulate too much inventory and receivables and to make unsound decisions on capital acquisitions.

There are two general ways to take account of capital employed. The older and still more common way is to express profits as a percentage of assets employed. Several conceptual and practical problems weaken the usefulness of this approach, of which the most important is that it motivates a high-profit division to reject investment opportunities that would lower its percentage return on assets employed, even though such investments might be profitable enough to increase the profitability of the whole company.[3]

Many of these weaknesses are overcome in the so-called residual income method, which was first adopted by the General Electric Company and is now used by a number of other well-known companies.[4] In this method, a capital charge is subtracted from profits computed in the conventional manner to give the final figure for residual income. The capital charge is calculated by multiplying the divisional assets by a specified percentage. The higher the residual income, the more the division is contributing to the company. The capital charge thus corresponds exactly to the interest cost of total capital as the term is used in this book.[5]

A full examination of the measurement of divisional profitability is inappropriate here. Special situations occur in which residual income can be misleading, and management must be alert to these. In addition, neither residual income nor any other single number can tell the whole story about a division.

When interest is included as an element of cost, the aggregate of the divisional income statements cannot readily be reconciled to the corporate income statement, because the latter excludes equity interest entirely and shows debt interest only as a general expense. If interest is included as a cost in inventory and in interdivisional transfers in the management accounting system, the problem of reconciling these numbers to the financial accounting numbers becomes even greater. Companies can, and do, use divisional profit measurement systems that are inconsistent with their financial accounting systems, but there are obvious advantages in having the two systems in harmony with one another.

Pricing

There are many situations in which selling price is arrived at outside the normal mechanisms of the marketplace. In these situations, the objective usually is to arrive at an equitable price, one that is equal to the seller's costs (as currently defined) plus a reasonable return on the capital he employs.

The difficulty that the Price Commission had in solving this problem and the solution recently adopted for arriving at a price on cost-type defense contracts were each discussed in chapter 4. Similar problems arise in pricing goods or services by individual businesses when the various products require different amounts of capital. Many businesses use cost-type contracts; negotiating such contracts would be simplified if both the buyer and the seller accepted the principle that interest is an element of cost.

In transactions that aggregate many billions of dollars a year, Blue Cross, insurance companies, and other third-party payers reimburse hospitals and other health care providers at an amount that supposedly approximates cost. The reimbursement would be both more equitable and more straightforward if interest were explicitly included as an element of cost.

Companies that operate on a job-shop basis, either because they manufacture to a customer's order or for other reasons, would find that pricing calculations that included an explicit allowance for interest would have marked advantages over a method that either ignores the amount of capital employed or a method that incorporates a crude approximation of interest. Indeed, the depressing effect on industry prices that results from the failure of some companies to realize what their costs actually are, might well be mitigated if it became common practice to include interest as an element of cost in arriving at selling prices.

Summary

Decision-makers often find that accounting information collected under existing principles is not the type of information they need. In some cases, managers create separate internal accounting systems that include interest as a cost element because they find that such systems provide useful information. But in a great many companies, the cost of operating two systems is so high and the problem of reconciling them so great, that management is unwilling to set up such a system. In these companies, mistakes can be made by relying on data from the conventional accounting system.

6

Measuring Interest Cost

Regardless of its conceptual merits, a proposal to record interest on both debt and equity capital as a cost has no practical significance unless it can be implemented. Two practical problems must be solved. First, and by far the more important, is the problem of measuring the interest cost of equity capital; this problem is discussed in the present chapter. Second is the largely procedural problem of deciding how interest cost should be incorporated in the accounts; this is discussed in chapter 7.

This chapter does not describe the one best method of arriving at interest cost, because I do not know what that method is. Rather, its purposes are to demonstrate that several feasible, objective methods of arriving at the interest cost do exist, and to suggest considerations that are relevant in deciding which of these methods should be adopted. Much further discussion is needed before a method is chosen.

Criteria

Interest cost is determined by applying a rate to the amount of capital employed. The amount of capital employed is easily determined; it is the book value of the assets employed for a cost objective. (Book value, rather than market value or any other value, is relevant because of the cost concept which is basic to accounting.) The problem arises in attempting to find the rate. More specifically, the problem relates to equity interest, for it is well accepted that debt interest costs can be measured. As is the case with all accounting practices, the method must satisfy three criteria:

1. It must be reasonably objective. Its results must not be greatly influenced by subjective human judgment. The results must be verifiable. On the other hand, the method need not be absolutely objective; many accounting practices require estimates of what will happen in the future or have other subjective elements.

2. It must measure approximately what the interest cost actually is. It need not do this precisely because few accounting measurements are precise.

3. It must be feasible. It must not involve such elaborate computations or depend on such expensive data gathering that the cost of applying the method exceeds its value. It must use information that is available when the accounting entries are made.

Debt Interest

As an introduction to the problem of measuring equity interest, it is useful to discuss some of the problems of measuring debt interest. The point of this discussion is that the problems of measuring debt interest are more serious than is commonly believed, but as accounting becomes more sophisticated, reasonable solutions to these problems are gradually being worked out.

For many years, accountants have dealt with the problem of measuring the cost of interest on bonds sold at a discount or at a premium, and the related problem of how to treat the call premium or unamortized discount when a bond issue is refunded. Not too many years ago a wide choice of methods was available. Bond discount or premium could be amortized on a straight-line basis; amortized on an annuity basis; or disregarded until the issue matured. The call premium that was paid when a bond issue was refunded could be counted as a cost over the remaining life of the old issue; counted as a cost over the life of the new issue; or charged directly to shareholders' equity, and thus not counted as a cost in any income statement. In recent years these options have been narrowed by pronouncements of the Accounting Principles Board. These pronouncements require that the income statement contain an approximation of the true annual interest cost.[1] The calculations required to arrive at this cost can be quite complicated.

In some circumstances convertible bonds are sold at a yield that is significantly less than the going rate of interest; the difference represents the value that investors place on the conversion privilege. When this occurs, the explicit interest cost is less than the true interest cost. The difference is not yet formally recognized in the accounts, but it does enter into calculations of earnings per share. The procedure set forth in *Opinion No. 14* of the Accounting Principles Board is complicated, but its complexity has not deterred the board from requiring it; nor has it deterred accountants from accepting the new requirement.

Some debt instruments are, on their face, noninterest bearing. It is apparent, since money is not borrowed without cost, that the face amount of the instrument includes both interest and principal, with the interest portion being hidden. The value of assets acquired with such an instrument would be overstated if they were booked at the face amount; they therefore should be booked at the true principal amount. In *Opinion No. 21*, the Accounting Principles Board requires that the imputed interest in such an instrument be separated from the principal, and that this interest should be recorded as a cost, just as if it were explicitly stated as such. Again, the problem of making such a separation is complicated, but this has not deterred the board from making a pronouncement.

Some land development companies sell land and accept in payment a mortgage that states an interest rate significantly below prevailing rates. In recording the revenue and the corresponding receivable in such a transaction, the accountant must estimate the true present value of the mortgage, and this requires, correspondingly, that he estimate an interest rate.

When a bank requires a compensating balance as a condition for making a loan, the true interest cost of the money that is actually made available to the company is higher than the rate of interest explicitly stated in the loan agreement. Although this element of interest cost is not currently recognized formally in the accounts, proposals for its inclusion are being considered by the Securities and Exchange Commission.

These examples show that the measurement of debt interest is not all that simple, that in various ways the accounting profession is moving in the direction of recording the true interest cost of debt, and that it is willing to accept quite complicated procedures in order to find the true interest cost.

The General Problem of Equity Interest Cost

There is no precise way to measure the interest cost of equity capital. "Cost of capital" has been a concept in public utility rate regulation since the nineteenth century, and it has been used in the analysis of important problems in industrial companies for about thirty years. Although hundreds of books and articles have addressed the problem, no one has come up with a practical solution, or at least no one has come up with a solution that is accepted by a large number of knowledgeable people.

The nature of the problem is as follows: In an artificial world in which a company paid out all its earnings as dividends, and in which earnings per share were stable over time, the dividend yield would be the cost of equity capital. If investors were willing, for example, to pay $100 for the privilege of receiving $10 in dividends annually, the cost of equity capital would be 10 percent. The real world, however, differs from this artificial world in two respects. First, most companies do not pay out all their earnings; instead, they retain a fraction of them (in some cases, all) with the expectation of putting these retained earnings to profitable use. Second, the stream of earnings is not stable; instead, it fluctuates from one year to the next for a number of reasons. Investors expect a higher return under conditions of risk and uncertainty than under conditions of relative certainty, as demonstrated by the fact that interest rates on government bonds are lower than interest rates on more risky industrial bonds, taking into account tax and length of maturity differences. The market price of a stock is influenced by investors' appraisal of these facts, but there is no exact way to measure how much of the price of a share of stock reflects the cost of equity capital, and how much of it reflects the market's judgment about the value of retained earnings and the company's prospects for future earnings.

In the voluminous literature on measuring the cost of capital, many approaches are suggested. In the special case of regulated companies, there may be a determinate solution, because there is a causal connection between the prices that these companies are permitted to charge and the cost of capital. For unregulated companies, however, the equations usually contain a symbol g, which stands for the estimated future growth of the company's earnings, and there simply is no objective way of finding a number to use for g.[2]

Practical Approaches

Despite these difficulties, businessmen do make judgments that involve, either explicitly or implicitly, a measurement of the cost of equity capital. Alternatively, they use a number that approximates the total interest cost for both debt and equity. Since the cost of debt interest is calculable, the cost of equity interest can be deduced if the total interest cost is known. Since these relationships will be used in the discussion that follows, an illustration is in order.

Table 6-1 shows the calculations of total interest cost in a company whose capital structure consists of 40 percent debt and 60 percent equity. The cost of debt capital is 4 percent. This is an aftertax cost because debt interest is tax deductible whereas equity interest is not; the two cost elements must be put on a comparable basis before they can be combined. If there are several types of debt capital with different costs for each, the 4 percent represents a weighted average of these costs. The cost of equity capital is 14 percent. (For the purpose of this illustration, we need not discuss where the 14 percent comes from.) By weighting each element's cost by the amount of that element, the total cost of capital, that is, the total interest cost, is shown to be 10 percent.[3]

In calculations of this type, the cost of debt capital is usually known within close limits; the problem is to find the cost of equity capital. From the relationships shown in table 6-1, it is apparent that this problem can be solved in either of two ways: (1) the cost of equity capital can be estimated directly; or (2) the cost of total capital can be estimated, and the cost of equity capital can be derived by making it the unknown term in the equation. Thus, if the total cost is estimated as 10 percent, and 1.6 percent of this is the weighted cost of debt, then 8.4 percent must be the weighted cost of equity; if equity capital comprises 60 percent of total capital, then the cost of equity is $8.4 \div 0.6 = 14$ percent.

Since the nineteenth century, an estimate of the cost of capital has been

Table 6-1
Calculating the Cost of Capital

	Amount	Weight	Cost	Weighted cost
Debt	$200,000	0.4	4%	1.6%
Equity	300,000	0.6	14%	8.4%
Total	$500,000	1.0		10.0%

an element in the calculation of rates for regulated public utilities. Some regulatory agencies have used the total cost approach; that is, they did not estimate the cost of equity capital separately, but rather set a cost for total capital, from which the implied cost of equity capital could be derived in the manner described. In recent years, this total interest cost has been in the neighborhood of 8 percent for all public utilities. The equity cost for an individual utility varied with the proportion of debt to equity in that utility.

The determination of an interest cost of total capital as a basis for setting rates is a different type of problem than that faced by a company whose prices are market based. In a utility, there is a self-fulfilling prophecy: the interest cost of equity capital comes out to be a certain amount because rates were set so as to yield that amount (neglecting the influence of regulatory lag and other factors that make actual net income different than that assumed in the rate-making calculations). Nevertheless, profits derived from these rates were high enough to attract capital to the industry, and this tends to validate the appropriateness of the 8 percent rate as the interest cost of total capital.

The majority of industrial companies use a required earnings rate, a required rate of return, or some comparable number in analyses involving proposed capital investments. Whatever its name, it is analogous to the total interest cost shown in table 6-1. A great many different methods are used to arrive at this number, but they will not be described here. For present purposes, the important point is that companies can arrive at a number they regard as sufficiently reasonable to use in analyses on which important business decisions are based.

Companies that use the residual income method of measuring divisional performance must compute a "capital charge" as one element of a division's cost—either as an interest cost, or as the sum of interest plus depreciation. In both, the interest component is conceptually the same as the interest cost proposed here.

These illustrations show that methods of arriving at an interest cost that includes both debt interest and equity interest are used widely. Opinion differs about how the calculations should be made, just as opinion differs about both the method of calculating depreciation on fixed assets and the useful life that is embodied in a depreciation calculation—but the calculations are in fact made. The dispersion of results from various methods of calculating total interest cost is not any greater than the dispersion of results from various methods of calculating depreciation.

Problems to be Resolved

With the foregoing as background, we can now discuss the problems that need to be resolved before the Financial Accounting Standards Board can issue a standard on accounting for interest cost. Such a standard would presumably describe how the interest cost of capital employed for various cost objectives should be measured. This cost would be determined by applying an interest rate to the amount of capital employed. Consistent with the cost concept that permeates accounting, the rate should be applied to the recorded cost of assets employed, rather than to their market value, and the rate itself should reflect current or historical cost, rather than an estimate of future cost. The rate should incorporate the costs of obtaining various types of capital, but the principal problem in arriving at the overall rate is to decide on the method of computing the interest cost of equity capital. Within this general framework, the following questions need to be answered:

1. Should the equity interest rates vary depending on the risk characteristics of individual companies?

2. Should the standard describe an interest rate for total capital, or should it focus on the interest rate for equity capital?

3. Should the FASB set a rate directly, or should it prescribe a method that each company will use to arrive at its own rate?

4. How should the rate be derived?

5. In computing total interest cost for a given year, should each increment of capital be costed at the rate applicable when that increment was obtained, or should all capital be costed at the current rates?

An Allowance for Risk?

As explained in chapter 2, it is conceptually possible to regard equity interest cost either as "normal" interest, that is, with the same rate applicable to all companies, or as a cost that reflects the risk characteristics of individual companies. The latter approach is much more difficult to make workable than the former.

There have been attempts to develop "beta coefficients" that measure the risk of certain securities,[4] but these coefficients are not directly translatable into a risk component of interest rates, and they have been applied only to securities that are actively traded. Many individual companies estimate their own equity interest cost, for purposes described in the preceding section, and these estimates do reflect the company's risk characteristics. However, these estimates are quite subjective, and there is no general agreement about the proper approach for making them.

It has been suggested that rates might be established for each industry that reflect the risk characteristics of that industry. For example, it has been estimated that the cost of equity capital is:

7-8 percent for regulated companies,

9-10 percent for companies in noncyclical industries,

11-14 percent for companies in cyclical industries.[5]

There are obvious practical problems in applying this approach. Some studies indicate that industry differences primarily reflect differences in accounting practices rather than differences in the innate risk characteristics of the industry. For example, the pharmaceutical industry is used as an example of an industry that has a high rate of return on capital employed, but the computed rate is affected strongly by the fact that companies in this industry usually consider their research and development costs as expenses of the current year. If they capitalized these costs, the indicated return would be lower than that currently reported. Studies made by Stauffer indicate that the book return on capital employed differs significantly from the economic return in the following industries: computers and business machines, liquor, mining, oil and gas production, pharmaceuticals, chemicals and pesticides, photographic and optical equipment, book publishing, tobacco products, homogeneous package goods (soap, cosmetics), film production, and forest products.[6]

Even if the effect of these accounting differences could be allowed for, there are great practical problems in defining industries in a way clear enough so that a company knows in which industry it belongs. There are also problems in allocating the capital of a conglomerate to the various industries in which it operates.

Research to find solutions to these problems would be worthwhile, but in the current state of the discipline, it does not seem likely, for the near future, that an operational technique can be developed to incorporate differences in risk characteristics into the equity interest rates. If no such technique can be found, the answer to the first question is clear: the equity interest rate should be a normal interest rate, one that reflects the cost of equity capital without an allowance for the risk characteristics of particular companies. Such a rate is similar to, but higher than, the prime lending rate for debt capital—that is, the rate at which banks will lend to their least risky industrial customers. It might by analogy be called the *prime equity rate*.

The prime debt rate is approximately the same throughout the United States; it does not vary by more than a small fraction of one percent. Rates for other types of loans do differ from one another considerably at one moment of time, and the essential reason for these variations is that transactions have different risk characteristics.

As pointed out in chapter 2, if this approach to the determination of equity interest cost is adopted, the reward for risk will be included as part of net income, rather than as interest. In other words, each company has a specified cost for the equity capital it uses in a given year, and its net income reflects how well it has performed after covering that capital charge. Approaches to finding the prime equity rate are discussed in a following section.

Total Capital or Equity Capital?

In rate regulation, some government agencies arrive at an interest rate for total capital; the rate for equity capital can then be deduced by the method illustrated in table 6-1. Similarly, for internal purposes, many companies estimate a rate for total capital employed. By analogy, it might be argued that the approach to the measurement of interest cost should be to prescribe a method of measuring total capital cost and let the rate for equity capital in a given company be obtained by deduction.

Such an approach has peculiar consequences, however. Table 6-2 shows calculations for four companies based on the assumption that the interest rate for total capital is set at 10 percent for all companies. The format is the same as that in table 6-1, but the calculations were made by taking the 10 percent as a given and working backward to derive the rate for equity capital. In several respects, the results seem odd. Company A has an implied interest rate on equity capital of 34 percent, as compared with the 11.5 percent rate of company B, simply because company A is highly leveraged. The proportion of debt to equity does indeed have some effect on the interest cost of equity, but it is not inevitable that a company with a high debt/equity ratio has a high equity interest cost. The high ratio may be entirely appropriate in the particular circumstances.

Even more striking is the contrast between Companies A and C and Companies B and D. These pairs of companies differ in that C and D are riskier than A and B, and this fact is reflected in a higher interest rate of debt. The calculations work out, however, to a lower equity interest rate in the risky companies, which does not correspond to common sense. Thus, despite the fact that the calculation of a total interest rate is common practice, it does not provide the correct approach for our present purpose. Instead, the interest rate for equity capital should be estimated directly.

Table 6-2
Effect of Single Overall Interest Rate

	A			B		
	Highly Leveraged			*Small Debt*		
	Weight	*Cost*	*Weighted cost*	*Weight*	*Cost*	*Weighted cost*
Debt	.80	4%	0.032	.20	4%	0.08
Equity	.20	34%	0.068	.80	11.5%	0.92
Total	1.00		0.10	1.00		0.10

	C			D		
	Highly leveraged risky			*Small debt risky*		
	Weight	*Cost*	*Weighted cost*	*Weight*	*Cost*	*Weighted cost*
Debt	.80	5%	0.04	.20	5%	0.01
Equity	.20	30%	0.06	.80	11.2%	0.09
Total	1.00		0.10	1.00		0.10

Prescribed Rate or Prescribed Method?

If researchers develop a feasible way of establishing a rate for equity interest that incorporates risk, then the FASB presumably would prescribe this method. If it is decided that the measurement of risk is not feasible and that equity cost should be derived from a prime equity rate, then the question becomes whether the FASB should prescribe this rate directly or whether it should prescribe a principle that would guide a company in arriving at its own rate.

The first alternative has the advantage of simplicity. After appropriate analysis, along lines discussed in the next section, the FASB would state that, effective on a certain date, interest on equity capital shall be computed at a rate of x percent. The rate would be changed in response to significant changes in interest rates in general. The difficult task of devising words that would clearly describe how each company should compute its own rate would be avoided. The conceptual justification for such an approach is that the rate intentionally excludes variations in risk characteristics among companies, for reasons discussed above, and that these variations account for the differences in the cost of equity capital among companies. This being the case, it is appropriate that all companies use the same rate.

Such an approach, however, poses two problems. First, the predecessor bodies to the Financial Accounting Standards Board never went so far as to prescribe a number as the solution to any problem; the closest they have come to this is to prescribe limits for, e.g., the maximum period over which goodwill should be amortized. With this precedent, the new board probably would be reluctant to prescribe a specific number. It might feel, with justification, that the business community would regard such a move as arbitrary. Second, it is not demonstrable that variations in equity interest rates are entirely associated with variations in a company's risk characteristics. This approach rests entirely on the plausibility of this assertion. since the reasoning is that the reward for risk can be treated as profit. Although the assertion *is* probably plausible, other forces may well be at work that can be identified and measured in a given company. More research on this point is desirable. If, for either of these reasons, the FASB decides that it should not prescribe a rate, then it must prescribe how companies should compute their own rate. Thus, this is one of the questions that, for the present, remains unanswered.

How Should the Rate Be Derived?

There are two possible approaches to the derivation of the equity interest rate: it can be related to some debt rate, or it can be derived independently.

Defliese suggests that the equity interest rate might be set equal to the debt interest rate, on the grounds that a company usually has the option either to borrow capital or to sell stock and that therefore the debt rate available at the time the equity investment is made is most appropriate.[7]

Arthur Andersen & Co. suggests that the cost of total capital to be allowed as a cost element on defense contracts might be calculated at a rate that is 150 percent of the current New York prime rate "to reflect prime borrowing rates plus allowances for compensating balances and prime rate premiums for the defense industry (bank risk rather than contractor risk)."[8]

Linking the equity interest rate to the debt rate would permit the equity rate to fluctuate with movements of interest rates in general. If this approach is adopted, further study would be required to establish the most appropriate relationship between the equity interest rate and the prime borrowing rate.

Alternatively, the prime equity rate could be estimated directly. Several empirical studies of this subject already exist, and they can be used as a starting point.[9] Generally, these studies were made for the purpose of finding the discount rate appropriate for use by the federal government; this rate should approximate the rate that the average taxpayer uses, because government investments use funds that otherwise would be invested in the private sector. The studies tend to show that the normal equity interest rate is relatively stable over time, and that it is in the neighborhood of 10 percent; but both conclusions need to be substantiated by further research.

Because no perfect way exists to separate the market value of stock into its two components—namely, the implied equity interest rate and the market's evaluation of the probability of growth in future earnings—the equity interest rate can never be calculated precisely. Experience with public utility rate regulation, the fact that the rate is necessarily higher than the debt interest rate, and the existing empirical studies all indicate that the appropriate rate is in the neighborhood of 10 percent.

Leonard Spacek supports a 10 percent equity interest rate:

Utilities are generally capitalized on about a 50-50 capitalization basis, as between equity and fixed carrying cost securities, such as debt. A composite debt rate of 6-8% and an equity rate of 10-11% produces an average rate of return for all capital. The lower rates of 6 and 10 are based on historical borrowings and capital raised, and the higher based on present rates. In the case of industrial companies, experience has shown that any industrial company that earns 10% on its capital results in its capital selling at approximately book value. Thus, at this point the total compensation to the owner is a recovery of use of capital without profit. If we adopted a procedure of allowing a total 10% cost of capital for all corporations and then deducting that portion of that total cost that was paid out in interest, we would get a balance of cost that would be applicable to equity. The amount applicable to equity would fluctuate in terms of a rate in relation to cost of that capital depending upon what percent of total capital was borrowed. For instance, if the capitalization of the company is 80% borrowed, the interest rate on the equity portion is very high—but it is not much in amount. I believe this method, while probably accurate, would not be nearly as well understood as adopting a 10% interest cost on equity capital across the board, and then allowing anything over or under as being a profit or loss in operation of the entity.[10]

Although empirical studies do support a rate in the neighborhood of 10 percent, these studies deal with *average* equity costs and therefore include an allowance for average risk. If the basic approach is that the equity interest rate is to be a *prime* equity rate, then the rate selected probably should be somewhat less than 10 percent, perhaps 8 percent. A relatively low rate would doubtless be more palatable to those concerned about possible abuses arising from the inclusion of interest as a cost, as described in chapter 3. On the other hand, the lower the rate, the less closely it corresponds to the real cost of capital and therefore the less useful it is in measuring divisional profit performance and for other internal purposes.

Although no attempt is made here to arrive at a definitive answer to the question of how the rate should be derived, it seems clear that a feasible, objective way of arriving at an interest rate for equity capital can be developed. The range of acceptable rates is not wide. The rate selected within that range will be an approximation, of course, but accounting contains many approximations: the write-off of intangible assets of uncertain life, the methods of assigning overhead to products and to segments of a corporation, and, above all, depreciation. There is increasing acceptance of the principle that it is better to make a reasonable approximation than to neglect the problem entirely, a principle that is applicable to the present problem.

Current Rate or Historical Rate?

The final problem to be examined is whether the equity interest rate applied to the amount of equity capital should be the rate in existence at the time the equity capital was acquired or whether the current rate should be applied to the total amount of equity capital used in the current year.

The cost concept, it would seem, provides an answer to this question: services are booked at their acquisition cost; therefore, the rate for a given amount of equity capital is the rate in force at the time that amount was acquired. The applicable interest rate on debt provides an exact analogy. Debt interest cost is derived from the rate agreed to when the funds were borrowed; subsequent fluctuations in the general level of debt interest rates do not affect the cost of that capital. (Borrowing when the cost is explicitly tied to the prime borrowing rate is an exception to this general rule.) Thus, if a company raises $10 million of equity capital in a year when the equity interest rate is 8 percent, the interest cost on that capital is $800,000 a year—as long as the company continues to use it.

To the extent that equity capital is acquired through retained earnings, the same principle would apply. The equity interest rate applicable to retained earnings would be the rate in existence during the year in which the earnings were retained.

There are, however, both conceptual and practical reasons for departing from the historical cost approach and using the current equity interest rate as the basis for assigning all equity interest cost in the current year. Conceptually, it can be argued that the decision whether to pay dividends or to use retained earnings in the business depends in part on the current cost of capital, not its historical cost. As a practical matter, it would be simpler to cost all equity capital at a single rate than to cost each year's increment separately, although this is a relatively trivial problem. It is also true that if each year's retained earnings are costed at the rate applicable to that year, an assumption would have to be made as to whether dividends were taken out of the pool of retained earnings on a Lifo basis or a Fifo basis. The Fifo basis seems the more plausible assumption.

Because of the merits of each side of this argument, no firm answer to this question is advanced here. It remains open for further study. If, however, the equity interest rate remains stable from one year to the next, as seems likely, the problem of choosing an applicable rate for a given amount of capital does not even arise.

Other Aspects of Measuring Equity Interest

Although the preceding questions are the principal ones that need to be resolved, a number of detailed problems must be addressed. Brief mention is made here of convertible bonds, preferred stock, deferred taxes, and other nonmonetary liabilities and equities.

If the market price of convertible bonds is significantly influenced by the conversion privilege, then capital raised through convertible bonds probably should be treated as equity capital for the purpose of calculating interest cost.

Capital raised from the issuance of preferred stock would normally be costed at its dividend rate, although it could be costed at the equity interest rate if it were participating preferred and if the market placed a value on the participation privilege.

The cost of capital obtained from deferred income taxes and similar liabilities is zero, and the amounts should be so stated in calculating the weighted interest rate to be applied to capital employed.

Reserves that are in effect retained earnings should be costed at the equity interest rate.

Nonmonetary current liabilities such as accounts payable and accrued liabilities probably should be excluded from the calculation, as not being a source of capital, and subtracted from current assets to give the amount of working capital for which capital is employed—but an alternative treatment is also possible.

Criticisms of the Approach

If it were necessary, one could develop in a few days a specific method for arriving at the interest rate, choosing from the alternatives given above. Before a single procedure is decided upon, however, there should be further discussion. Advocates of the status quo seize on the existence of these alternatives, and particularly the fact that no approach will provide the precise interest cost, as convenient reasons for dismissing the whole proposal.

The same criticism was made some fifty years ago to the proposal to incorporate depreciation in accounting.[11] As with interest, the amount of depreciation cost is an estimate, and alternative ways of recording depreciation on identical assets were permitted when depreciation accounting first became accepted, and indeed are still permitted today.

Critics reject the analogy with depreciation, however, on the grounds that in the case of depreciation, one starts with the cost of the asset, which is a known amount, and the problem is merely to distribute a portion of this amount to each of a number of years. There is, they say, no correspondingly firm starting point for measuring equity interest cost. Also, no check on the validity of the method corresponds to the check that can be made by comparing the net book value of an asset with the proceeds at the time of its disposal.

This criticism of the depreciation analogy is, in my opinion, not valid. In measuring equity interest cost, one starts with a known amount: the amount of equity capital, as recorded in the accounts. The problem is not to distribute this amount to each of a number of years, but rather to estimate a rate that reflects the cost of using it in a given year. This is not conceptually any more difficult than the problem of deciding how much of the cost of an asset should be charged as depreciation in a given year. It is unlikely that the range of error in the estimate of equity cost will be greater than the range that results from differences about what method of depreciation is appropriate, compounded by differences as to the useful life of the asset, and compounded further by differences about which expenditures represent maintenance expense and which should be capitalized.

Advocates for the status quo are also concerned that no practical solution is suggested here for the problem of incorporating an allowance for risk in the equity interest cost. Without such an allowance, some say, the rate does not measure the true cost of equity capital; therefore, it is worthless. It does not follow, however, that a less than perfect measure is worthless, for worth varies along a continuum. A measure that did incorporate risk would be more useful than one that did not, but a measure of the "prime" equity interest cost is more useful than the omission of this cost entirely. The approach to interest cost suggested here is not arbitrary; it is based on a sound concept, and on a practical way of making that concept operational. The prime equity interest cost has a useful and understandable meaning—the minimum cost of equity—and it explicitly follows that the reward for risk is incorporated in the net income amount. If a practical way of incorporating risk could be developed, this would be fine, but some reasonable way of incorporating interest cost seems preferable to the alternative of ignoring the undeniable fact that interest is a cost.

Experience in the federal government on a somewhat similar problem is relevant. For fifteen years or more, there have been discussions about the discount rate that should be used in benefit-cost analyses of proposed government investments. Books, articles, and innumerable internal memoranda have been written advocating one approach or another. Proponents of various approaches have argued their views at formal conferences and informal meetings. Finally, on March 27, 1972, the Office of Management and Budget issued Circular A-94, announcing, in effect, a moratorium on the argument. From now on, it instructed, everyone should use a rate of 10 percent. To some, this solution appears arbitrary, but it *is* a solution; it is a simple solution, the rate selected has sound analytical support, and it permits agencies to get on with their job without the frustrations and delays occasioned by arguments over the proper rate.

Because of the impossibility of obtaining an exact measure of equity interest cost, some argue that the interest charge should be based only on the interest cost of debt. As indicated above in connection with the defense contract problem, this would result in an accounting system inferior to that which we now have. The interest cost of cost objectives is related to the *amount* of capital employed for those cost objectives, not to the *source* of that capital. A system that incorporated only debt interest assumes that equity capital has zero cost, which is not the case. The effort should be to measure the cost of using capital, whatever its source.

Finally, a few critics question my reliance on the cost concept in accounting. They point out that the calculation of equity interest cost gives no weight to the current market value of the company's stock (except in a year in which a company obtains capital by a common stock issue). The fact is that the current market value of a company's stock has no more bearing on its equity interest cost than the current market value of its bonds has on its debt interest cost. In both cases, the cost was established at the time the capital was acquired.

Summary

This chapter has explored the feasibility of arriving at an equity interest rate, which is the principal problem that must be solved in order to account for interest cost. All the details for measuring the interest cost of equity capital have not been developed here, and some questions have been left unanswered. Certainly, much more study is required before an accounting standard is promulgated. The analysis, however, does seem to substantiate the feasibility of arriving at a reasonable rate.

As a minimum, based on studies already available, the Financial Accounting Standards Board could publish a rate that companies would be expected to use unless they could demonstrate that an alternative rate was better. This rate would be an approximation, but its use would be preferable to ignoring the equity interest cost entirely. Beyond this minimum, the FASB could initiate research that would lead either to a better overall rate or to a standard set forth in sufficient detail so that companies could objectively arrive at a rate applicable to their situation.

7

Accounting Procedures

If one accepts the fundamental proposition that interest is a cost and that it should be treated similarly to the way other elements of cost are treated, most of the procedures for working interest cost into the financial accounting system are easy to determine by analogy. The general principles are:

1. An interest rate is determined annually by dividing total annual interest cost by the amount of capital employed.

2. In most circumstances, the interest cost assigned to a cost objective is found by multiplying the capital employed for the cost objective by this interest rate.

3. The interest cost of capital assets used in the manufacturing process is an element of product cost and is assigned to products in the same way that depreciation on plant and equipment is assigned.

4. Interest is an element of the cost of newly acquired plant and equipment. The cost includes the interest cost of the capital assets used in constructing plant and equipment, the interest cost of other capital tied up during the construction process, and the interest cost of advance payments or progress payments on purchased plant and equipment.

5. When assets are held in inventory for significantly long periods of time, interest cost is an element of the cost of these assets.

6. That portion of the interest cost for a year that is not assigned to cost objectives in accordance with the above principles is a general expense of the year.

7. The annual equity interest cost is credited to retained earnings.

Calculation of the Interest Rate

A company obtains capital from various sources, some from banks, some from bond issues, some from other creditors, some from equity investors, and some from retained earnings. In general, the capital obtained from each source is best thought of as flowing into a common pool. Although the right-hand side of the balance sheet shows the sources of capital, and the left-hand side shows the assets in which capital has been invested, there usually is no direct connection between an individual item on the right-hand side and an item on the left-hand side.

Although the purchase of a building may be financed in part by a mortgage loan associated with that specific building, the existence of this loan affects the overall capital structure of the company. Any significant addition to debt affects the overall borrowing capacity of the firm. Even in these circumstances, therefore, it is preferable to think of the capital as flowing into a common pool rather than as associated with a specific asset. Thus, as a general rule, the interest cost for each item of capital employed should be calculated at an interest rate that represents the weighted average cost of *all* capital.

Table 7-1 shows a method of calculating this interest rate. The total annual interest cost is calculated in section A, according to the principles suggested in chapter 6. (Recall that the cost of debt interest is its aftertax cost.) The total capital employed is calculated in section B. The interest rate is obtained by dividing annual interest cost by total capital employed.

Both the sources of capital and the assets in which this capital is employed are listed at their book amounts. It might appear that the effect of this is to distort the cost of shareholders' equity if the market value of shareholders' equity is significantly different from its book value, which often is the case. That no distortion in fact results can be seen by examining the relationship between the sources of capital (section A) and the uses of capital (section B). The assets are recorded at their cost, and the sources of the capital used to acquire these assets are also recorded at their cost as of the time the capital was acquired. The current market value of the shareholders' equity does not affect the book value of the assets employed, and it likewise should have no effect on the amount used to calculate equity interest cost. The total sources of capital listed in section A should equal the total uses of capital in section B. Unless the whole approach to accounting shifts to a market-value basis, the cost principle should be followed.

The interest cost calculated in section A of table 7-1 is in the nature of an *interest pool*, similar to other overhead cost pools. Amounts are to be credited from this pool and charged to applicable cost objectives, as described below.

The debit to the interest pool for debt interest is calculated at the aftertax rate, since debt interest is a tax-deductible expense. The difference between this aftertax cost and the actual interest cost on debt would be debited to a tax adjustment account. The debit for equity interest should be at its calculated rate, since this cost is not tax deductible. Admittedly, the notion of incorporating tax effects into product costs is unusual. It has become customary to record extraordinary gains and losses at their aftertax amount, and this practice has some similarity with that recommended for debt interest. The alternative of recording debt interest at its pretax cost and equity interest at double the stated amount would be another way of solving this problem, but an impractical one, because the resulting rate would be unreasonably high, and the interperiod tax allocation problem

Table 7-1
Calculation of Interest Rate ($000 omitted)

A. Annual Interest Cost

	Amount	Aftertax rate	Interest cost
Interest on short-term borrowings	$ 400	5%	$ 20
Interest on bonds, Series A	1,000	4%	40
Interest on bonds, Series B	2,000	5%	100
Nonmonetary liabilities	600	0	0
Preferred stock	1,000	9%	90
Common shareholders' equity	5,000	9%	450
Total	$10,000		$700

B. Capital Employed (i.e., Assets)

	Amount
Current assets	$ 3,000
Less current liabilities (net of $400,000 short-term borrowings)	−1,000
Monetary working capital	2,000
Noncurrent assets (at book value)	8,000
Total capital employed	$10,000

C. Calculation of Interest Rate

$$\frac{\text{Annual interest cost}}{\text{Capital employed}} = \frac{\$700}{\$10,000} = 7 \text{ percent}$$

would become quite complex. In any event, the treatment of debt interest and equity interest must be consistent; either both should be aftertax, or both should be pretax.

Possible exceptions to this general rule need to be considered: (1) a possible distinction between working capital and permanent capital, and (2) assets financed with capital uniquely associated with these assets.

Working Capital

It can be argued that the capital used to finance inventory and other current assets costs less than the capital used to finance plant and equipment and other noncurrent assets. Working capital turns over rapidly, and the company therefore has less exposure to risk than in the case of fixed assets, in which the capital is effectively locked up for a period of many years. This has led some companies, in their internal accounting systems, to make a lower charge for working capital than for permanent capital. The new pricing principles of the Department of Defense (chapter 4) make a similar distinction. Some companies may therefore decide that there should be two rates for calculating the interest cost to be applied to cost objectives: one for inventory and the other, and higher, rate for noncurrent assets.

Specific Financing

Although in general it is not appropriate to associate sources of capital with specific uses (as in the case of mortgage loans mentioned above), there may be instances in which such an association is desirable. For example, if a company finances raw material inventory at low cost because of favorable credit terms extended by suppliers, or if inventory is in part financed by progress payments, it may be desirable to vary the corresponding interest charge accordingly. These situations need to be analyzed individually, to determine whether the relevant interest cost does differ from the company average, and if so, whether it differs materially. These are, in any event, exceptions to the general rule.

Charging Interest to Cost Objectives

Depreciation on assets used in the manufacturing process becomes part of the cost of manufactured products. It therefore is part of the inventory cost of these products and appears on the income statement as part of cost of sales when the products are sold. Depreciation on assets used in marketing, administrative, and other nonmanufacturing activities is charged as an expense of the current period.

Analogous procedures would be used for interest cost. Interest on the capital used in the manufacturing process becomes part of the cost of manufactured products; as such, it is included in the inventory cost of these products, and it appears on the income statement as part of the cost of sales when these products are sold. Interest on capital used in marketing and administrative and other nonmanufacturing activities is charged as an expense of the current period.

The same mechanism used to assign depreciation to products could be used to assign interest to products. Indeed, there are advantages in using a single "capital charge" that combines both depreciation and interest in a single number. As demonstrated in chapter 5, if depreciation is calculated by the annuity method, the capital charge for a given asset would be equal in each year of its life and would match the implicit assumption about the assignment of investment costs to products that underlies many calculations of the profitability of proposed capital investments. In such profitability calculations, the recovery of capital and the charge for the use of capital are considered together.

In connection with the calculating of profits on the basis of capital employed, the Department of Defense has developed detailed techniques for associating interest costs with contracts. These techniques are set forth in Defense Procurement Circular 107, which is summarized in Appendixes A, B, and C. Companies can easily adopt these techniques to their own needs.

In addition to the interest cost associated with depreciable assets, a charge for the capital tied up in land, which is a nondepreciable asset, is included in product costs.

An Alternative Procedure. In the procedure described above, interest is *not* added to plant, equipment, or any assets other than inventory after these assets have been acquired. Interest is a charge for the *use* of capital. It is a cost or expense in the year in which these assets are used, and is charged to appropriate cost objectives in that year. Defliese, by contrast, suggests a system in which interest cost is added to the book value of the assets each year, and the depreciation charge is calculated on the basis of this book value.[1] In his system, interest cost reaches the final cost objectives as a part of the depreciation charge. This approach can be structured so that it gives exactly the same result as that suggested above. It can be used, of course, only for depreciable assets.

New Plant and Equipment

The principles of cost accounting apply not only to products manufactured for sale but also to assets constructed by a company for its own use. Interest cost on the plant and equipment used in constructing such assets is an element of their cost. So, too, is the interest cost of capital tied up by the company during the construction process if it is a significant amount, which it is likely to be for major construction projects. By the same token, if the company uses its own capital on construction projects performed by outside contractors, as is the case when it makes advance payments to such contractors, the interest cost on such capital is an element of the cost of the project.

The general rule is that the cost of an asset includes all elements of cost that are involved in bringing the asset to the point in place and time where it is ready for productive use. Interest is one of the elements of such cost.[2]

Costs of Carrying Inventory

Conceptually, an interest cost is associated with holding assets in inventory. If the manufacturing cycle is short, the cost may not be significant enough to warrant the effort of assigning an interest carrying cost to products. When the passage of time is itself a significant part of the production process, however, interest cost is important enough to record. Examples include the accretion of lumber and fruit trees, tobacco, distilled liquor, and petroleum.

As pointed out in chapter 3, this procedure would not lead to inflated inventory amounts because the lower-of-cost-or-market rule sets a ceiling to inventory amounts, and this rule would remain in full force. The actual effect should be to bring inventory amounts for assets that are held for long periods of time up to levels that more closely approximate their cost to the company.

Monetary Assets

Should interest cost be assigned to monetary assets such as cash, accounts receivable, and short-term investments? The answer depends on whether one makes a sharp distinction between the nature of monetary and non-monetary assets. If one takes the view that nonmonetary assets are essentially unexpired costs, and that the function of accounting is to match these costs with the appropriate revenues, then interest cost probably should be associated only with nonmonetary assets. If no such distinction between monetary and nonmonetary assets is drawn, an argument can be made for assigning some interest cost to monetary assets, although such a practice may well have no material effect on net income.

Interest Expense

The total interest cost for a year, on both debt capital and equity capital, is debited to an "interest pool" account, as described in a preceding section. This account is credited for the interest cost that is assigned to cost objectives according to the procedures described above. The balance in the account represents unassigned interest cost. It represents a general expense for the year, just as do other elements of cost not assigned to specific cost objectives. As with these other elements of cost, the unassigned interest cost becomes part of the general and administrative expenses of the year and would be so reported on the income statement.

For reporting the performance of divisions or other segments of the company, unassigned interest cost can be treated in the same way as other elements of general corporate expense. Some companies prefer not to assign this expense to divisions at all. Other companies assign some or all of general corporate expense to divisions on some reasonable basis. In the case of interest expense, the reasonable basis would be the amount of assets employed by the division.

Debits to the Interest Pool

Under the proposed method, some of the interest costs incurred in a period are credited out of the interest pool and wind up in plant, inventory, and other asset accounts; the remainder is a general expense of the period. What about the debits to the interest pool? What credit entries should offset these debits?

With respect to the debt interest component of interest cost, the problem of disposing of the credit is purely mechanical. The amount of debt interest, either paid in cash or accrued, is recorded as a part of normal transactions, and the credit entry offsetting the debits mentioned above would correspond to these transactions. For example, if all debt interest cost were collected in a debt interest account, the credit would be to this account, in an amount that equals its debit balance.

With respect to the equity interest component, the problem is more complicated, and three solutions have been proposed: credit interest income, credit retained earnings, or credit a new shareholders' equity account.

Although crediting equity interest to interest income is currently the practice in public utility accounting, it is *not* consistent with the basic premise of our proposal. It is a holdover from the outmoded proprietary theory of accounting. Recognition of equity interest does *not* create income; on the contrary, it discloses an element of cost. Furthermore, if this treatment were permitted, the resulting net income amount would be practically the same as it is in current practice; the only difference would be the timing differences that arise when interest is included in capitalized amounts. Thus, the net income would not convey the message that it is the amount left after the cost of capital has been recognized. (The variation of making the credit to the account for debt interest expense, up to the balance of this account, has the same net effect and has even less justification.)

Both the second and third alternatives show the credit as an increase in the shareholders' equity, which is what it is, and both bypass the income statement, which should be done. Both have the effect of reporting the increase in shareholders' equity that arose because of the normal charge for the use of the shareholders' capital, as distinguished from the increase resulting from profitable operations. The credit is not "earnings," in the same sense that profits are earnings, and the creation of a new account in the shareholders' equity section is therefore a more descriptive way of disclosing the facts. It is not clear, however, that the balance sheet separation of the increase in shareholders' equity that arose from the capital charge and the increase that arose from profits (in the economic sense) provides sufficiently useful information to warrant making it. It also raises the problem of how dividend payments are to be divided between the two accounts.

In any event, the credit in the shareholders' equity section shows the amount of capital that shareholders have permitted to remain invested in the company's assets because they did not withdraw the cost of using that capital. It is equivalent to the credit in the bondholders' account that arises when the interest they have earned has not been paid to them. Thus, although both the second and third alternatives are conceptually sound, the practice of making the credit directly to retained earnings is the simpler of the two.

Under current practice, retained earnings are credited for the amount of net income. In the new procedure, there are two entries: a credit for the equity interest cost; and an entry for profit or loss, which could be either a credit or a debit depending on whether or not the company was able to earn more than its equity interest cost.

Other than the one adjustment described above, the entries for income tax expense remain unaffected. Income taxes are computed as prescribed by the Internal Revenue Service, and it is assumed that these requirements will not change (although there are arguments in favor of such a change, as discussed in chapter 4).

APB *Opinion No. 9* requires that substantially all increases in retained earnings be reported on the income statement. With the proposed new definition of net income, the credit for equity interest obviously could not be shown as an item that enters into the determination of net income. Adequate disclosure can be achieved, however, by reporting this item "below the line," in a manner illustrated in the next section.

Other Procedural Problems

How should interest income and other earnings on investments in other companies be recorded? Interest income on loans or bonds would continue to be recorded at the amounts earned. For equity investments, the equity method continues to be applicable for those situations in which it is specified. For equity investments for which the so-called cost method is specified, it may be more desirable to record equity interest income, as computed in the preceding section, than to record only the amount of dividends earned.

Questions also have been raised about the treatment of equity interest by insurance companies, banks, and other financial institutions. No attempt is made here to deal with these special situations. Only in recent years have these institutions begun to keep their accounts in a way that even approximates the generally accepted principles that apply to industrial companies. Those persons who have done such an excellent job of bringing accounting in financial institutions into the twentieth century can undoubtedly find a practical way of incorporating interest costs into this accounting.

The procedure may require an entry for deferred income taxes. This problem is seen more clearly in the next illustration, and discussion of it is deferred until then.

An Illustration

Table 7-2 shows a condensed set of financial statements, structured so as to highlight the changes that would occur if the proposal were adopted. Each change will be discussed. Throughout, it is important to remember that the contrast depicted in table 7-2 is the situation in the year of transition. In subsequent years, the effect may be different, and these differences are also discussed briefly.

Transactions affecting the Interest Pool are shown in table 7-3.

These entries should be interpreted in the following way: Debt interest and equity interest were added to the pool. The actual cost of debt interest was $20, and its aftertax cost was half this, or $10; the other $10 was debited to a tax adjustment account. The equity interest cost was $30, making the total interest cost $40. This $40 was disposed of by the following transactions: $31 was charged as a cost of products manufactured, and by the end of the year $23 of this cost has flowed through to cost of sales and $8 remained in product inventory; $4 was added to the cost of new plant; and $5 was not assigned to cost objectives and therefore became a general expense of the year.

The effects of these transactions on items in the income statement are:

1. *Cost of sales* increases by the interest component, $23, that was included as an element of cost. In future years, cost of sales would always be higher than under current practice because of the inclusion of interest.

2. Selling, general, and administrative expenses are reduced by the $20, which, under current practice, was the amount of debt interest expense, and it was increased by $5, the amount of interest expense that was not assigned to cost objectives—a net decrease of $15.

Table 7-2
Financial Statements under Current and Proposed Principles

	Income Statement			
	As currently reported		*As proposed*	
Sales revenue		1,000		1,000
Cost of sales	680		703	
Selling, general and administrative	220		205	
Tax adjustment	0	900	10	918
Income before taxes		100		82
Income tax expense		50		50
Net income		50		32
Total interest cost			40	
Less debt interest cost (after taxes)			10	
Equity interest cost				30
Addition to retained earnings				62

	Ending Balance Sheet		
Assets			
Inventory		150	158
Plant and equipment (net)		300	304
Other assets		300	300
Total assets		750	762
Liabilities and shareholders' equity			
Current liabilities		150	150
Long-term debt		250	250
Capital stock		100	100
Retained earnings		250	262
Total equities		750	762

Table 7-3
Interest Pool Transactions

From debt	10	To cost of sales	23
From equity	30	To inventory	8
		To plant	4
		To general expense	5
	40		40

3. *The tax adjustment* item is shown separately here to account for the tax effect of debt interest. In practice, other ways of showing this item might be more informative.

4. *Income tax expense* has not been changed in the example. The effect of the proposal on income tax transactions depends on: whether or not the debt interest that is capitalized in asset amounts will nevertheless be allowed as a current tax-deductible expense; whether equity interest will be allowed as a deductible expense; and practice with respect to interperiod tax allocations. Because different assumptions would lead to different results, and in the interest of simplicity in exposition, no adjustment at all was made. If taxable income is increased by the capitalization of debt interest, there will be a corresponding increase in income tax expense. In the example, it would be 1/4 of the capitalized interest cost of $12, multiplied by the income tax rate (assumed to be 50 percent), which comes out to $1.50. The income tax effect is largest in the year of transition. Income tax expense will *not* be affected by the recognition of equity interest, unless the tax statutes are changed, because the difference between accounting income and taxable income that arises from equity interest is a permanent difference rather than a timing difference.

5. *Net income* decreases by $18. Essentially, this is because equity interest has been included as an element of cost, but the amount does not correspond to the $30 amount of equity interest cost, because $12 of equity interest cost has become lodged in asset accounts. In future years, net income will be lower under the proposed method than under the present method because of the inclusion of equity interest as an element of cost.

6. *Inventory*, on the balance sheet, increases by $8, which is the amount of interest included as an element of cost in products that have been manufactured but not sold. On future balance sheets, the same phenomenon will operate to make inventory amounts higher than they would have been under current practice.

7. *Plant and equipment* increases by $4 because of the inclusion of interest as an element of cost in new plant assets. (The balance sheet does not reflect a revaluation of existing assets in order to avoid distorting the overall effect of the transition. In any event, such a revaluation is probably not worth the trouble of making it.)

8. *Retained earnings* increases by $12. This is the net effect of two changes, as follows:

	Present	*Proposed*	*Difference*
Net income	$50	$32	$−18
Equity interest	0	30	+30
Total additions	$50	$62	$+12

Net income is lower under the proposed method, but this is offset by the amount of equity interest. In the year of transition, these two changes do not offset one another, because of the addition of equity interest to inventory and plant accounts. This is essentially a one-time phenomenon. In future years, the total additions to retained earnings should be approximately the same under the proposed method as under the present method, subject only to fluctuations in the amount of capital employed in inventory and plant.

In summary, the changes are:

1. Cost of sales increases, because of the inclusion of interest as an element of cost.

2. Net income decreases, because of the recognition of equity interest, which under current practice does not appear as an element of cost or expense.

3. Certain asset amounts increase, because of the inclusion of interest as an element of cost.

4. After the year of transition, the total credit to retained earnings will be approximately unchanged, as compared with the present method, but the total will comprise two elements: equity interest and net income.

8 Implementation

Gaining acceptance of a fundamental change in accounting principles is difficult, but by no means impossible. The most significant change in this century was the recognition of depreciation. Although double-entry accounting has been in existence for more than four hundred years, depreciation accounting was not generally used until the late nineteenth and early twentieth centuries. Its use was fostered by the Revenue Act of 1913, which permitted a depreciation deduction for income tax purposes. By the 1930s depreciation was universally recognized in the United States as a proper expense to be included on the income statement.[1] No informed person today questions that depreciation is a cost.

The current mechanism for setting accounting principles poses a problem that did not exist in the 1930s, however. Accounting principles are supposed to have "substantial authoritative support." Up to now, this support has been demonstrated by the evidence that many companies did follow a certain practice in their own accounting. Thus, the job of the standards-setting body (until 1973, the Accounting Principles Board; now, the Financial Accounting Standards Board) was to bless one or more of several existing practices. But as the standards-setting body continues in its admirable effort to narrow the range of acceptable alternatives, it will soon run out of topics on which it can make such choices. Soon, the board will be unable to look to actual practice for promising innovations, because the board's own rules will prohibit innovations that it has not approved in advance.

As a practical matter, the board cannot experiment with proposed changes by *suggesting* that companies prepare supplementary financial statements that incorporate the proposed change and then by observing their results. This approach was tried for price-level accounting, but the public record shows that only a handful of companies in the United States accepted the suggestion, and those companies subsequently abandoned it.

It is also a fact that the APB tended to act only when there was a crisis. When abuses of revenue realization came to light in the case of franchise and real estate development companies, but not before, new rules were promulgated. No crisis is involved in the present proposal. On the other hand, the Financial Accounting Standards Board is new. The report of the Trueblood Committee has stimulated accountants to think of fundamental matters.[2] In this atmosphere, the FASB may be willing to tackle a new proposal, even if it is not associated with a crisis.

The proposal made here involves a fundamental change both in the definition of net income and also in the amounts at which certain assets will be reported on the balance sheet. As noted in chapter 2, a few companies already have adopted some of the practices suggested, and their financial statements are consequently inconsistent with those of other companies. It would be unfortunate if these practices spread haphazardly, for this would increase the difficulty of making comparisons among companies. Thus, it is highly desirable that the FASB act fairly promptly.

At the same time, it is recognized that the proposal requires more research and a great deal of discussion before the FASB is in a position to act on it *in toto*. This suggests that it would be desirable to develop a way of implementing the proposal in stages, with early stages involving relatively modest changes in current practice.

Of the various possibilities for a step-by-step approach, that of starting with specific types of items in specific industries is perhaps the most attractive. There is precedent for this. In recent years, new standards have been published that apply only to banks, only to insurance companies, only to extractive industries, or only to nonprofit organizations. What parts of the present proposal are amenable to such special treatment?

Companies that hold inventory for long periods of time come immediately to mind. The approach is relatively easy to apply to such inventories, and it would have a significant effect on the financial statements of these companies. The standing timber of lumber companies is a good first candidate. The asset increases in value with the passage of time, but the increase is inadequately recognized under present accounting methods. The inclusion of interest as an element of cost would help to bring the inventory amount in line with reality. The oil reserve of petroleum companies is another possibility. These reserves appear on the balance sheets of many companies at ridiculously low amounts; the inclusion of an interest cost would make balance sheet amounts correspond more closely to reality and would reflect more accurately what actually is happening to shareholders' equity in such companies. Inventories that are aged for several years, such as tobacco and distilled liquor, are other possibilities. The first pronouncement could well be limited to situations of this type.

Next, or at the same time, the FASB could require that interest be included as an element of cost in self-constructed plant and equipment. This practice, with respect to debt interest, is already followed by public utility companies and by some industrial companies; it would be simple to extend it to all companies. As a transitional device, this has the advantage of acquainting users of financial statements with the basic idea that the use of capital does have a cost, and that this cost should be recorded in the accounts.

The general adoption of other aspects of the proposal, as described in the preceding section, could be deferred until the two steps described above have become well accepted and well assimilated.

Appendixes

Appendix A
Summary of Defense
Procurement Circular 107[a]

Working Capital

DPC 107 incorporates two distinct methods for estimating the working capital requirements of a contract: the "Historical Data Method" and the "Projected Method." It should be noted that the distinction here is between the computational methods used and is not necessarily related to the nature of the data employed in those computations. Thus, both methods could be applied to "actual" as well as to "projected" cost data.

This historical method proceeds on an annual basis. If the computation deals with projections, as is the case with DFC 107, the average amount of operating capital employed by a profit center in the performance of federal government contracts during a selected annual period, such as the most recent fiscal year, must be first established. This average amount of capital is then related to total annual costs incurred by the profit center to establish "net operating capital employed factors." These factors are in turn applied to projected total contract costs to obtain the estimated amount of operating capital required for the performance of each contract. The calculation must be separately performed for all the profit centers that make charges to a given contract. They are made on Form 1858, as described in Appendix B. The calculation for a profit center is made on section I of Form 1858, and a summary is prepared for each contract on section II. This summary provides an estimate of the total amount of operating capital needed over the entire life of the contract. It should be noted that if the procedures were applied to "actual" cost data, a separate computation would become necessary for each year during the performance of a given (long-term) contract.

The alternative projected method is not described in detail here. In this method, the calculations are not directly linked to any organizational unit, such as a profit center, but are made individually for each contract. Basically, the method seeks to establish the cash-flow patterns associated with each contract; the amount to be invested by the contractor is thus computed in a somewhat more direct manner than with the historical method. The projected method can clearly be applied both to actual and to projected accounting data.

[a]This summary is adapted from a paper prepared by the Staff of the Cost Accounting Standards Board as a part of the board's research into the issues related to recognition of the cost of using capital in connection with negotiated defense contracts.

In dealing with the selection of methods, it should be noted that DPC 107 specifies that the contractor should generally use the historical method applied to historical data to develop his capital employed factors. The use of the projected method, using projected data, is limited to certain specific circumstances outlined in the circular. However, since all of these computations are envisaged only as part of developing a profit objective for contract negotiations, the application of the technique to "actual" costs is not really contemplated.

Composition of Operating Capital

Whatever the method employed in measuring operating capital requirements of a contract, the amount so measured must be based on a sound and unequivocal definition of "operating capital." DPC 107 defines operating capital as "the net current assets necessary for financing the performance of Federal Government contracts." This definition is elaborated upon in the instruction governing the application of the historical method (Form 1858), which shows the following items as components of operating capital:

1. average federal government contracts accounts receivable balances;

2. average contract gross inventory balances including raw materials, supplies, work in process and finished goods inventories committed to federal government contracts. (Pooled inventories that support both government and commercial work should be allocated.)

3. Progress payments, advances, reimbursements, and credits should be subtracted from the gross inventory balances to arrive at average net inventory investment.

4. Trade accounts payable are specified as the outstanding balances of "outside" vendor, supplier and subcontractor billings, for purchases and subcontracts covering materials, components, and services.

All other current assets and liabilities are excluded from the calculation under the historical method. In particular, any cash balances and prepayments are excluded on the asset side and correspondingly "nontrade payables and accruals, e.g., payrolls, taxes, insurance, contingencies and fees" are excluded on the liabilities side. The exclusion may be justified on the grounds of materiality (particularly if only the net effect after the offset between assets and liabilities is taken into account), or alternatively it could be argued that the excluded items are not really "necessary for financing the performance of Federal Government contracts." At any rate, some assessment of the propriety of DPC 107 selection procedures in this area seems appropriate.

The above discussion of the composition of operating capital was carried out in the context of the historical method. To be on a par with the historical method, the analysis of working or operating capital flows under the projected method should also embrace accounts receivable, net inventories (including an appropriate share of any "pooled" raw materials inventories), and trade accounts payable. Whether these items are actually included, however, depends on the interpretation placed on the term "cost incurred," since this expression is generally equated with commitment of operating capital. Thus, if it implies that an item of cost is recognized as being part of a contractor's operating capital only after it has been charged to a specific government contract, then clearly no allowance is made for any investment in common or "pooled" inventories. Therefore, if comparability is to be maintained between the two methods, some clarification is necessary as to how the "pooled" inventories can be properly taken into account in the case of the projected method. Establishment of inventory turnover rates for various types of inventories seems to be a prerequisite for any other steps in this direction.

Facilities Capital

"Facilities capital" is defined in DPC 107 as

tangible fixed assets (i) based in the regular business activities of a profit center, (ii) not intended for sale, (iii) capitalized on the books in accordance with the contractor's accepted accounting system, and (iv) that, except for land, are subject to an allowable depreciation or amortization expense in accordance with the contractor's accepted accounting system.

The basic procedure is given in Appendix C. In summary, the net book value of assets associated with a "profit center" is first determined. In this context, no distinction is made between assets used for commercial purposes and for government contracting. These assets are then distributed to "productive burden centers" within the profit center. By applying the appropriate imputed interest rate to assets so distributed, a total annual dollar amount of imputed interest cost for productive burden centers is computed. Since productive burden centers are defined in DPC 107 as "the accounting level within a profit center for which overhead rates are calculated," the overhead allocation base can be used to establish a "facilities capital imputed interest factor." For computational purposes, the latter may be regarded, in effect, as an addendum to the overhead rate, i.e., whenever an overhead rate is employed for pricing purposes, a second multiplication is carried out applying the "facilities capital imputed interest factor" to the appropriate overhead base associated with a given contract.

Valuation and Composition of Facilities Capital

DPC 107 stipulates that only tangible assets be included in the asset base. Consequently, all intangible assets, whether subject to amortization or not, are excluded. Also, assets are to be included in the base only if "used in the regular business activities of a profit center." More specifically, "the inclusion or exclusion of net book value for capital employed determinations small be consistent with the allowability of unallowability of costs generated by those facilities, for overhead and pricing purposes." Therefore, items such as idle capacity or facilities, as defined in ASPR, and plant under construction are excluded if no allowable costs are generated by those items. Leased assets are included only "when constructive costs of ownership of such fixed assets have been allowed in lieu of rental costs."

DPC 107 recognizes that part of a profit center's "facilities capital" may be "an allocable share of general purpose assets . . . which are held, or controlled by the corporation outside the profit center." Thus, any assets that qualify as "facilities capital" at the home office or at some corporate service center can be allocated to profit centers or segments if the costs generated by those assets are so allocated. Cost Accounting Standard 403 could be used as a guide for this cost allocation process.

However, at the profit-center level these costs, plus any other G&A costs incurred at this lower level, are commonly charged to contracts or other final cost objectives on some broad basis, such as total cost input. The charge is through a G&A rate, and thus the whole overhead computation process is bypassed. Therefore, the adoption of a rule specifying that "'undistributed' facilities are allocated to productive burden centers on any reasonable basis that approximates the actual absorption of the related costs of such facilities" seems to imply that a separate imputed interest calculation may be necessary to cover those assets whose depreciation charges become part of the G&A rate. Such a computation would be performed on the profit center basis without any allocation of assets to productive burden centers. Whether such a separate imputed interest computation should be introduced with respect to assets whose costs are recovered through the G&A rate is at least partly a question of materiality. And the answer to that question may in turn depend on prevailing fixed asset recording practices—particularly among the larger corporate entities.

In addition to being charged as part of overhead or G&A, depreciation is sometimes charged as a direct cost to final cost objectives or contracts. Where this is the case, a problem similar to the one described above in connection with the G&A rate seems to arise, i.e., the question will be whether a separate imputed interest rate to be employed in parallel with such direct charges of depreciation should be developed.

Appendix B
DPC 107—Operating Capital Determination

Historical Data Method

1. DD Form 1858 "Profit Center Historical Operating Capital" shall be utilized by contractors to report the required account average balances recorded in the Profit Center's historical accounting records separately for cost type and fixed price type contracts for both prime and subcontract Federal Government business. This financial data shall include transactions attributable to all Government subcontracts being performed by the Profit Center.

2. Section I of DD Form 1858 will normally be completed by a contractor annually, within 60 days following the close of the contractor's last completed fiscal year, and shall be used by all DOD procurement activities to estimate operating capital requirements for the entire performance period of a contemplated contract action. Section II of DD 1858 shall be completed by the Contracting Officer using his own cost objectives at the time of the pre-negotiation profit evaluation. For definitization of a letter contract, the latest complete contractor fiscal year available at the time the definitive contract is negotiated shall be used to estimate the Operating Capital requirements for the entire performance period of the contract.

3. *Annual costs incurred* are to be reported separately for cost and fixed price type contracts. *Annual costs incurred* are the total costs allowed or allowable under ASPR Section XV, Part 2.

4. All Federal Government work shall be included in calculating the amounts reported on DD Form 1858.

Profit Center Historical Operating Capital Instructions (DD Form 1858)

Purpose. This form has two sections. The purpose of the first section is to determine the operating capital historically required by each Profit Center in performing the federal government contracts, in terms of a factor per dollar of costs incurred. The purpose of the second section is to determine the estimated operating capital required to perform a specific contract or procurement action, by application of the appropriate historical factor to the contract estimated or proposed costs.

PROFIT CENTER HISTORICAL OPERATING CAPITAL		Form Approved O.M.B. No. 22R0306

CONTRACTOR: ABC, Inc. PROFIT CENTER: Vehicle Division ADDRESS:	FISCAL YEAR ENDED 12-31/71

SECTION I

GROSS OPERATING CAPITAL REQUIRED (Federal Government Contracts Only)		CONTRACT TYPE	
		FIXED PRICE	COST REIMBURSEMENT
AVERAGE ACCOUNTS RECEIVABLE		A 1,100,000	B 2,200,000
AVERAGE GROSS INVENTORY		C 20,200,000	D 18,000,000
LESS PROGRESS PAYMENTS, ADVANCES, REIMBURSEMENTS AND OTHER CREDITS		E 15,150,000	F 18,000,000
AVERAGE NET INVENTORY INVESTMENT	C-E D-F	G 5,050,000	H 0
AVERAGE CONTRACT INVESTMENT	A+G B+H	I 6,150,000	J 2,200,000
ANNUAL COSTS INCURRED (By Contract Type)		K 30,000,000	L 20,000,000
GROSS OPERATING CAPITAL EMPLOYED FACTORS	I÷K J÷L	M ● 205	N ●110

FINANCING BY TRADE ACCOUNTS PAYABLE		TOTAL PROFIT CENTER	FEDERAL GOVERNMENT CONTRACTS
AVERAGE TRADE ACCOUNTS PAYABLE		O	P 1,500,000
ANNUAL COSTS INCURRED	R = K+L	Q	R 50,000,000
ACCOUNTS PAYABLE FINANCING FACTOR	O+Q P+R	S ●	T ● 030

NET OPERATING CAPITAL EMPLOYED FACTORS		FIXED PRICE	COST REIMBURSEMENT
FIXED PRICE CONTRACTS	M-T or S	U ● 175	
COST REIMBURSABLE CONTRACTS	N-T or S		V ● 080

SECTION II

CONTRACT OPERATING CAPITAL (Complete for each Procurement Action)	RFP/CONTRACT PIIN NUMBER		CONTRACT TYPE
PERFORMING PROFIT CENTERS	CONTRACT ESTIMATED COSTS	NET OPERATING CAPITAL EMPLOYED FACTORS	ESTIMATED OPERATING CAPITAL REQUIRED
	W	X ●	Y
		●	
		●	
OPERATING CAPITAL - TOTALS	Z		A'

DD FORM 1 SEP 72 **1858**

36

Figure B-1. Defense Procurement Circular # 107: DD Form 1858

Basis. The Profit Center operating capital data and factors should represent actual experience in the latest complete fiscal year, for federal government contracts or subcontracts and by the two principal types. Therefore the effects of commercial (non-government) production is excluded.

Net Operating Capital. Net operating Capital Employed Factors represent the net investment after subtracting financing by Trade Accounts Payable.

Heading. Identify the contractor, Profit Center and Fiscal Year to which the historical data pertain.

Section I

Average Accounts Receivable (A&B). Enter the average federal government contract accounts receivable balances. Normally the sum of the monthly balances divided by twelve, although unusual billing or payment patterns may require more detailed analysis to determine a representative average.

Average Gross Inventory (C&D). Determine average contract gross inventory balances, by a monthly or more frequent method. Include raw materials, supplies, work in process and finished goods inventories committed to federal government contracts. Pooled inventories that support both government and commercial work should be allocated on a usage or other equitable basis.

Progress Payments, Advances, Reimbursements, Credits (E&F). Enter any credit balances recorded separately, that offset and reduce the contractors investment in inventories.

Average Net Inventory Investment (G&H). This is the average net investment after offsetting the above credit balances. If the contractor's system nets credits directly in the accounts, this average may be determined directly from the accounts, i.e., omit the "Gross" and "Credit" steps.

Average Contract Investment (I&J). The sum of Average Accounts Receivable and Average Net Inventory. These totals should reflect the contractor's average operating capital investment in each type of government contract.

Annual Cost Incurred (K&L). Enter the total annual costs incurred by the Profit Center on each type of contract. Cost unallowable under ASPR

Section 15, and uncontracted costs (eg., contractor's share of cost-sharing contracts) must be screened out so that these values are the same that flow through the above Accounts Receivable and Net Inventory.

Financing by Trade Accounts Payable

Average Trade Accounts Payable (O&P). Trade Accounts Payable are the outstanding balances of "outside" vendor, supplier and subcontractor billings, for purchases and subcontracts covering materials, components and services. Exclude non-trade payables and accruals, e.g., payrolls, taxes, insurance, contingencies and fees. Isolate Federal Government Contract payables if possible (P). Otherwise enter the Total Profit Center payables (O).

Annual Costs Incurred (Q&R). Enter total annual costs that correspond to the above Trade Accounts Payable. Government costs incurred (R) is the sum of the two contract types (K&L).

Accounts Payable Financing Factor (S&T). The quotient of Average Trade Accounts Payable divided by Annual Costs Incurred.

Net Operating Capital Employed Factors (U&V). The result of the Gross O.C. Factors (M&N) less the appropriate A/P Financing Factor (T or S). This represents the contractor's net operating capital employed for each dollar of cost.

Section II
Contract Operating Capital

Timing & Identification. This section is completed only when estimating the operating capital requirements for an individual procurement action. Identify the specific RFP/Contract PHN number and the contract type.

Performing Profit Centers and Contract Costs. List all Profit Centers expected to perform the contract, and enter the Contract Estimated Costs (W) to be incurred by each. The Total Costs (Z) must agree with the DD 633 cost proposal.

Net Operating Capital Employed Factors (X). The selection of the appropriate Net Operating Capital Employed Factor is determined by (a) the Profit Centers listed, and (b) the current Contract Type. Collect the latest historical data on Section(s) I for each Profit Center and determine the contract type for the current procurement action.

Estimated Operating Capital Required (Y). The product of Profit Center estimated costs (W) times the appropriate Operating Capital Factor (X). Sum the Profit Center requirements to arrive at the contract total operating capital (a).

Note to DD Form 1858

1. This historical method for estimating working capital is a much easier method for estimating operating capital in most instances. It is intended to be prepared annually by the contractor not more than 60 days after the close of his fiscal year and can be audited by DCAA at the same time as data is audited for Forward Pricing Rate Agreements (where FPRA's are used). For the second and successive contracts involving a profit center in a fiscal year, the information in section I should be available.

2. Information on payables specifically for Federal Government Contracts should be used if available, because it is more relevant. In many instances it will not be available and information for the profit center can be used as a substitute. The DD 1858s in the example have entries under the "Federal Government Contracts" heading (labeled P, R, & T). Had this not been available, entries O, Q, and S would have been used. The same Accounts Payable Financing Factor (either entry S or T) is subtracted from both fixed price and cost reimbursable Gross Operating Capital Employed Factors to arrive at the Net Operating Capital Employed Factors for the respective contract types.

3. Section II is prepared in accordance with the instructions on the form. It must be filled out for each contract action by the contracting officer. Since operating capital allocated depends on the cost estimate used, operating capital estimates used by contractors and contracting officers will differ by a factor reflecting the different cost estimates used. Section II—DD 1858 reflects the contractor's cost estimate and the operating capital factors developed. The PCO's "markup" using his own cost estimates is made separately.

Appendix C
DPC 107—Facilities Capital Determination

Facilities Capital

a. Facilities Capital to be reported includes land, buildings, machinery, equipment, vehicles, tools, patterns and dies, furniture and fixtures, and similar capitalized property having a physical or bodily substance. All reported Facilities Capital shall be classified into one of the categories as described below:

(i) *Land*—Includes non-depreciable real estate and related non-depreciable improvements and property rights, including land leasehold improvements that are subject to amortization.

(ii) *Buildings*—Includes depreciable real estate and related depreciable improvements, including building leasehold improvements that are subject to amortization.

(iii) *Equipment*—Includes all reported Facilities Capital other than that classified as Land or Buildings, including all improvements not included in (i) or (ii) above that are subject to amortization.

b. The estimate of Facilities Capital to be employed in the performance of a proposed contract action is derived from ''Overall Profit Center'' facilities capital data projected by the contractor.

c. DD Form 1860 ''Profit Center Facilities Capital Projection'' shall be used by the contractor to project estimated book values of fixed assets to be employed by a Profit Center in the conduct of all its business, including non-Federal Government work. A separate Form 1860 shall be prepared for each contractor fiscal year during which Government contract performance is anticipated. Regardless of whether a contractor submits operating capital data on DD Form 1858 or 1859, DD Form 1860 shall be used for Facilities Capital projections. Submission of Forms 1858 and 1860 will be initiated under the same circumstances as Forward Pricing Rate Agreements (see 3-807.12(b)), and will normally be submitted and evaluated as complementary documents and procedures. If this procedure is not applicable, submissions may be made annually or with individual contract pricing proposals, as agreed to by the contractor and the cognizant ACO.

d. Facilities Capital to be reported for this purpose shall include only those tangible fixed assets (i) used in the regular business activities of a Profit Center, (ii) not intended for sale, (iii) capitalized on the books in accordance with the contractor's accepted accounting system, and

(iv) that, except for land, are subject to an allowable depreciation or amortization expense in accordance with the contractor's accepted accounting system. Leasehold improvements (as distinguished from the lessor's real or personal property) and ADP system software that meet the criteria of (i) through (iv) above shall be reported as Facilities Capital. All other recorded intangible fixed assets, either subject to amortization (e.g., patents, copyrights, franchises), or not subject to amortization (e.g., goodwill, trademarks) shall not be reported as Facilities Capital.

e. Facilities Capital is the total net book values of: (i) all contractor-owned fixed assets recorded on the books of the Profit Center, (ii) all leased fixed assets, under control of the Profit Center, when constructive costs of ownership of such fixed assets have been allowed in lieu of rental costs, and (iii) an allocable share of general purpose assets of the nature of (i) and (ii) above which are held, or controlled by the corporation outside the Profit Center. Net book values reported for each year are after amortization and depreciation allowable under Section XV, Part 2, and are the average of the beginning and ending final year balances. The reported net book values of facilities available to a contractor for less than a full fiscal year's depreciation, or amortization should be reported on an annualized basis.

f. The projection of facilities (land, buildings, and equipment) book values and overhead allocation bases is an integral part of a contractor's overhead rate forecasting process. Therefore, projections of Facilities Capital data and allocation bases on DD Form 1860 shall be consistent with the data base used by a contractor for overhead rate forecasting. For example, net book values of fixed assets reported on DD Form 1860 shall be the same values that generate related depreciation expenses in projected overhead pools, and the Facilities Capital allocation bases shall be reconcilable with the bases projected for overhead rate pricing purposes.

g. If a Forward Pricing Rate Agreement for overhead rates has been negotiated, the inclusion or exclusion of net book value for capital-employed determinations shall be consistent with the allowability or unallowability of costs generated by those facilities, for overhead and pricing purposes. For example, if costs of excess facilities have been disallowed in forward pricing rates, the value of those same facilities shall be excluded from the capital base. The file shall contain similar information relative to the overhead and Facilities Capital allocation bases. When audited overhead data are used for contract pricing, both the audit report recommendations and subsequent contract pricing negotiations shall treat the facilities values and allocation bases reported on DD Form 1860, and the related facilities expenses and bases contained in the overhead rate(s) proposal on a consistent basis.

h. In either of the above methods for allocating indirect expenses to individual contracts, overhead rates often are arrived at on an "overall" basis, i.e., without settlement of individual elements of the overhead cost proposal. Under such circumstances it will be necessary, when establishing a contract profit objective, for the Government negotiators to estimate any adjustments to the proposed Facilities Capital data considered appropriate. Also, when an advance agreement covering the cost of idle facilities or idle capacity exists for a contractor Profit Center, the fixed asset values reported on DD Form 1860 shall be consistent with the provisions of such agreement.

i. Leased property is a special case. If full rental costs have been accepted in overhead pools, no capitalized value shall be recognized. If rental costs have been limited to the construction cost of ownership, the constructive value of the leased property shall be recognized. When contractors enter into a long-term lease of property whereby the conditions of such lease require the advance payment by the tenant to the lessor of the total rental amount for the cumulative term of the lease, such prepaid rental payments made by the contractor under a long-term lease shall be treated similarly to contractor-owned fixed assets and a capitalized value of the prepayment shall be included in the category of "Leased Property" on the DD Form 1860, provided that the lease payments are otherwise reported for each year shall be the average of the prepaid lease account for the year, except when such leased facilities were available for only a portion of the year; in those circumstances, an annualized (see *e* above) prepayment amount shall be reported. In the event any leased fixed assets are included as Facilities Capital, a separate attachment to DD Form 1860 shall show the following information:

    i. Description of the asset
    ii. Initial valuation of leased property and basis for value
    iii. Amortization Schedule
    iv. Net book value included on DD Form 1860
    v. Identification of Government authority and date when determination was made to allow only the constructive cost of ownership for the asset, in lieu of full lease or rental costs. (Not applicable in case of prepaid leases.)

j. A Profit Center is defined for this purpose as the lowest accounting level (e.g., division, plant, product line) for which the balance sheet items of accounts receivable, inventory, accounts payable, and tangible fixed assets (land, buildings and equipment) are available.

k. A Productive Burden Center is the accounting level within a Profit Center for which overhead rates are calculated for distribution of indirect costs. The Productive Burden Center structure listed on DD Form 1860 shall be compatible with that used for pricing purposes on the contractor's cost proposal (DD Form 633). DD Form 1860 shall include all Productive Burden Centers in the Profit Center, without regard to the proportions of Government and commercial business involved. Contractors utilize various methods of overhead pooling and distribution bases, sometimes with multiple allocations between pools. When an elaborate overhead allocation system is utilized, or when there are a large number of Productive Burden Centers within a Profit Center, contractors are encouraged to consolidate and simplify allocation of Facilities Capital to a limited number of allocation bases. However, any consolidated structure used shall be compatible with the contractor's cost breakdown, so that consolidated Facilities Factors can be equitably applied to appropriate contract allocation bases (see DD Form 1861).

l. Service or support centers are cost centers for the collection of costs for performing specific functional services, e.g., data processing center, plant services, administrative services, or wind tunnel facility. The fixed asset values of service or support centers whose costs are allocated to contracts through a G&A expense rate may be treated similarly to a Productive Burden Center or handled in accordance with the "undistributed" definition below. When service or support center costs are occasionally charged direct to customers on a use charge basis, e.g., computer direct charge, the fixed asset values shall be handled similarly to a Productive Burden Center as defined above.

m. Distributed Facilities is the net book value of all fixed assets that are identified in the plant records as *wholly assigned to a Productive Burden Center*. Such identification usually results in related charges (e.g., depreciation or taxes) direct to the using burden center. When some costs of a service or support center are charged direct to customers on a "use charge" basis (e.g., computer center), the assets of such center shall be allocated between "distributed" and "undistributed" assets in the ratio that the service or support center direct charges bear to the indirect charges.

n. Undistributed Facilities is the net book value of all fixed assets which are not specifically assigned to a Productive Burden Center (e.g., housekeeping and general service equipment, land, or general plant buildings), and that portion of corporate fixed assets that are allocable to the Profit Center (e.g., general office equipment, corporate headquarters, and land). Undistributed assets are allocated to Productive Burden Centers on any reasonable basis that approximates the actual absorption of the related costs of such assets.

o. Allocation Bases are the direct input bases (e.g., direct labor dollars, direct labor hours, direct material dollars or machine hours) projected to be incurred in or by each Productive Burden Center (including service or support centers) for the purpose of allocating overhead costs or use charges. As stated in paragraph f above, the estimated allocation base projected for the capital employed computation shall be consistent with the base projected for estimating overhead expense rates of each burden center. In addition, when a Productive Burden Center allocation base estimated for overhead rate purposes normally includes the efforts to be expended in the accomplishment of IR&D and B&P tasks, the allocation base for this profit on capital computation shall exclude such efforts. Such allocation base exclusions (e.g., engineering direct labor dollars, model shop direct labor hours) shall be consistent with the estimated amounts of these bases used in establishing the allowable costs under either an advance agreement or a formula computation.

Profit Center Facilities Capital Projection Instructions
(DD Form 860)

Purpose. The purpose of this form is to (a) project and accumulate total facilities values for each Profit Center by contractor fiscal years, and (b) to reduce those values to Facilities Capital Employed Factors applicable to the total Overhead Allocation Base of each Productive Burden Center.

Basis. All data pertains to the same fiscal years for which the contractor prepares capital budgets and overhead projections, and should be compatible with both of those procedures. More specifically, facilities values projected here should relate to facility—generated costs proposed or allowed in overhead rate projections.

Identification. Identify the contractor, profit center, address and fiscal years to which the data pertains. Sufficient fiscal years must be projected to cover the estimated performance periods of contracts to be negotiated.

Definitions. See ASPR 3-808-7(e)(3)(i) for definitions of the facilities values to be included, the different sources and classes of those values, the distinction between Distributed and Undistributed facilities, and definitions of Productive Burden Centers and Overhead Allocation Bases.

Productive Burden Centers. List every Productive Burden Center within the Profit Center for which overhead rates are calculated for the allocation of indirect costs. The structure reported must be compatible with that used in DD 633 cost proposals or supporting detail.

114

PROFIT CENTER FACILITIES CAPITAL PROJECTION
Form Approved O.M.B. No. 22R0306

CONTRACTOR: ABC, Inc.
PROFIT CENTER: VEHICLE DIVISION
ADDRESS:

CONTRACTOR
FISCAL YEAR: 1972

		1. ACCUMULATION AND DIRECT DISTRIBUTION			2. ALLOCATION OF UNDISTRIBUTED			3. TOTAL NET BOOK VALUE (Col's 1 + 2)			4. OVERHEAD ALLOCATION BASE	8. PROJECTED FACILITIES CAPITAL EMPLOYED FACTORS (Col's 3 ÷ 4)		
		LAND a	BLDGS b	EQUIPMENT c	LAND a	BLDGS b	EQUIP c	LAND a	BLDGS b	EQUIP c	Base Unit of Measure*	LAND a	BLDGS b	EQUIP c
PROFIT CENTER	RECORDED	200	2,300	3,490										
	LEASED PROPERTY				Basis of Allocation:									
	CORPORATE	40	150	100	Analysis of distribution of related overhead.						DL$			
	TOTAL	240	2,450	3,590										
	UNDISTRIBUTED			100										
	DISTRIBUTED	240	2,450	3,490										
PRODUCTIVE BURDEN CENTERS	Engineering			115	66	669	27	66	669	142	1,800	.03666	.37166	.07788
	Manufacturing			3,375	174	1781	73	174	1781	348	4,800	.03625	.37104	.71833

FISCAL YEAR 1973

		1. ACCUMULATION AND DIRECT DISTRIBUTION			2. ALLOCATION OF UNDISTRIBUTED			3. TOTAL NET BOOK VALUE			4. OVERHEAD ALLOCATION BASE	8. PROJECTED FACILITIES CAPITAL EMPLOYED FACTORS		
		LAND a	BLDGS b	EQUIPMENT c	LAND a	BLDGS b	EQUIP c	LAND a	BLDGS b	EQUIP c		LAND a	BLDGS b	EQUIP c
PROFIT CENTER	RECORDED	200	2,200	3,495										
	LEASED PROPERTY													
	CORPORATE	60	330	200							DL$			
	TOTAL	260	2,530	3,695										
	UNDISTRIBUTED			100										
	DISTRIBUTED	260	2,530	3,595										
PRODUCTIVE BURDEN CENTERS	Engineering			335	47	461	18	47	461	353	1,200	.03916	.38416	.29416
	Manufacturing			3,260	213	2069	82	213	2069	3342	5,400	.03944	.38314	.61888

FACILITIES NET BOOK VALUE*

PRODUCTIVE BURDEN CENTER

*Enter all dollar values to nearest thousand.

DD FORM 1860
1 SEP 73

Figure C-1. DD Form 1860

Land, Buildings, Equipment. "Land" is nondepreciable realty, improvements and property rights. "Buildings" is depreciable realty and related improvements. "Equipment" is all depreciable property other than Buildings.

Recorded, Leased Property, Corporate. "Recorded" facilities are the normal Fixed Assets owned by and carried on the books of the Profit Center. "Leased Property" is the capitalized value of leases for which constructive costs of ownership have been allowed in lieu of rental costs under ASPR 15-205.34 & .48. The government determination must be identified. "Corporate" facilities are the Profit Center's allocable share of corporate-owned and leased facilities. All of the above are summed on the "Total" line which represents the Profit Center's total facilities values recognized for this purpose.

Direct Distribution. (Col's 1a, b, c). All facilities values that are identified in the plant records as wholly assigned to or located in Productive Burden Centers, are listed against the applicable P.B.C. Detail is totaled upward to the Profit Center "Distributed" line. Profit Center "Undistributed" is the remainder of the P.C. "Total." Both source and distribution of Profit Center facilities values must balance at the "Total" line.

Allocation of Undistributed. (Col's 2a, b, c). Profit Center "Undistributed" facilities are allocated to Production Burden Centers on any reasonable basis that approximates the actual absorption of the related costs of such facilities. This allocation will usually reflect the method of allocating G&A and/or Service Center costs for the purpose of computing overhead rates.

Productive Burden Center Total Net Book Value. (Col's 3a, b, c). The sum of Col's 1a, b, c, & 2a, b, c. Total each class of facility separately, and prove back to the Profit Center "Total."

Overhead Allocation Base. (Col 4). The direct input bases (e.g., DL$, DLH, DMS, M-H, etc.) projected to be incurred in or by each P.B.C. (including service/support centers) for the purpose of allocating overhead or use charges. Identify each base unit-of-measure, which must be compatible with the bases used for applied overhead in DD 633 cost proposals or supporting detail. Quantities must agree with negotiated overhead rates for forward pricing purposes or FPRAs (ASPR 3-807.12).

Projected Facilities Capital-Employed Factors. (Col's 5a, b, c). The quotients of the P.B.C. Total Net Book Values (Col's 3a, b, c) separately divided by the P.B.C. Overhead Allocation Bases (Col 4) Carry each

Factor to three decimal places, e.g., X.X.X.X. This Factor represents the amount of Facilities Capital required to support each unit of the Overhead Allocation Base.

Notes to DD Form 1860

1. The basis of allocation of undistributed assets in each profit center between the engineering productive burden center and the manufacturing productive burden center (located under Item 2) should be related to the manner in which the expenses generated by these assets are absorbed in the overhead rate. The choice of the basis for allocation is up to the contractor within the limits stated above. The base unit of measure in the allocation base (column 4) is determined by his accepted method of overhead allocation. In the example, the basis for allocation of undistributed assets assumes an analysis was made of overhead distribution. These bases for allocation must be consistent for all fiscal years during which the contract will be performed.

2. The sum of the entries in Column 2a for the engineering and manufacturing burden centers is equal to the entry in the undistributed line, Column 1a. The same relationship holds for Column 1b and 2b and 1c and 2c.

3. The base unit of measure used for allocation in Column 4 refers to all work done in a productive burden center, not government work alone.

4. The average of the beginning of year and end of year values is used to determine asset values for DD 1860. When an asset has not been or is not expected to be owned for an entire year, an annualized asset value is used.

5. This form is submitted annually, and projections must be consistent with capital budgets and the overhead rate projections of the submitting corporation. Should these budgets be revised significantly up or down between annual submissions, a new set of DD 1860's should be submitted reflecting the changes.

Instructions
(DD Form 1861)

Purpose

The purpose of this form is to compute the estimated Contract Capital Turnover Rate, as an index of capital employed on the Contract. An intermediate step is to determine the facilities capital to be employed in

CONTRACT CAPITAL EMPLOYED

CONTRACTOR: ABC, Inc.			RFP/CONTRACT PIIN NO.
PROFIT CENTER: VEHICLE & CONTROLS DIVISIONS			N00099-72-R-99999
ADDRESS:			PERFORMANCE PERIOD 3/1/72 - 9/30-73

1. PROFIT CENTERS PRODUCTIVE BURDEN CENTERS	2. FISCAL YEARS	3. CONTRACT OVER-HEAD ALLOCATION BASES	ESTIMATED FACILITIES CAPITAL EMPLOYED					
			4. FACILITIES FACTORS			5. FACILITIES AMOUNTS		
			LAND (a)	BLDGS (b)	EQUIP (c)	LAND (a)	BLDGS (b)	EQUIP (c)
VEHICLE DIV.								
Engineering	1972	62 DL$	.0367	.3717	.0789	2	23	5
	1973	8	.0392	.3842	.2942	-	3	2
Manufacturing	1972	115 DL$	.0363	.3710	.7183	4	43	83
	1973	525	.0394	.3831	.6189	21	201	325
CONTROLS DIV.								
Engineering	1972	190 DL$	.0269	.2856	.0825	5	54	16
	1973	40	.0264	.2786	.1014	1	11	4
Manufacturing	1972	190 DL$	.0271	.2871	.6800	5	55	129
	1973	270	.0263	.2750	.5825	7	74	157

6. CONTRACT FACILITIES CAPITAL EMPLOYED		45	464	721
7. CONTRACT OPERATING CAPITAL EMPLOYED	DD Form 1858 or 1859	870		
8. TOTAL CAPITAL EMPLOYED	Sum Lines 6 + 7	2100		
9. CONTRACT TOTAL ESTIMATED COST	DD Form 1547	5000		
10. CONTRACT CAPITAL TURNOVER RATE	Line 9 + 8	X 2 ● 381		

DD 1 FORM SEP 72 1861

Figure C-2. DD Form 1861

each Profit Center and Productive Burden Center, using the Facilities Factors developed on DD Form 1860.

Heading

Complete the identification data at the top of the form. The Performance Period determines the Facilities Factors, by Fiscal Year, that must be used in the computations.

1. Profit Centers and Productive Burden Centers. List the contractor Profit Centers and Productive Burden Centers that will perform work on this procurement action. The breakdown is extracted from the cost proposal shredout, price analysis report and/or audit report, and correlate to the facilities breakdown used on DD Form 1860.

2. Fiscal Years. For each of the above organizational elements, breakout the Fiscal Years of performance by each. This breakout is secured from the same source as the above.

3. Contract Overhead Allocation Bases. For each Productive Burden Center and Fiscal Year, enter the amount of the related Allocation Base used to derive the contract estimated total cost. These bases should be the same as those used for burdening contract overhead. The base units of measure (e.g., DL$, DLH, DMS, etc.) must agree with those used in Col. 4 of DD Form 1860.

4a, b & c. Facilities Capital Employed Factors. Carry forward the appropriate Facilities Factors from Col's 5 of DD Form 1860. Profit Centers, Productive Burden Centers and Fiscal Years must agree.

5a, b & c. Facilities Capital Employed Amounts. The products of each Contract Overhead Allocation Base (3) times its related Facilities Factors (4a, b & c).

6. Contract Facilities Capital Employed. Sum the above to determine the total facilities capital employed, by class.

7. Contract Operating Capital Employed. Carry forward the Operating Capital from DD Form 1858 or 1859.

8. Total Capital Employed. The sum of all classes of capital employed (lines 6 & 7).

9. Contract Total Estimated Cost. The total estimated or proposed cost, or cost objective, for the contract. For a contractor, this must agree with his DD Form 633 cost proposal. For a procurement contracting officer, with his DD Form 1547, total cost objective.

10. Contract Capital Turnover Rate. The quotient of Contract Total Estimated Cost (9) divided by the Contract Total Capital Employed (8).

Notes

Chapter 2
Conceptual Foundations

1. Lloyd G. Reynolds, *Economics: A General Introduction* (Homewood, Ill.: Richard D. Irwin, 1963), pp. 118-19. In reviewing a number of textbooks in order to illustrate the above point, I was struck by how little attention authors gave to the difference between the economics concept of interest and the accounting concept as reflected in published financial statements. Typically, an author will call attention to the fact that "profit" on a financial statement is a mixture of interest and true profit, but he does this only in passing. None of the books I looked at pointed out that interest, unlike the cost of other factors of production, was never included in the measurement of the cost of products manufactured. Moreover, in the structure of the National Income Accounts, which was created by economists, the word "profit" is used to include interest on equity capital, just as the accountant uses this term. It is not surprising that some students who have taken a Principles of Economics course have difficulty in reconciling what they learned there with "real life" as expressed on accounting financial statements. See John W. Kendrick, *Economic Accounts and Their Uses*, (New York: McGraw-Hill, 1972), pp. 210, 211; and "Relation of Corporate Profits, Taxes, and Dividends in the National Income and Product Accounts to Corresponding Totals as Tabulated by the Internal Revenue Service," *Survey of Current Business* (July 1969).

2. In 1903 the shares of only thirty-seven industrial companies were listed on the New York Stock Exchange, according to Arthur Andersen & Co., *AICPA Study on Establishment of Accounting Principles* (Chicago, 1972), p. 27.

3. Norton M. Bedford, Kenneth W. Perry, and Arthur R. Wyatt, *Advanced Accounting: An Organizational Approach* (New York: John Wiley & Sons, 1961), p. 4.

4. For discussions of the entity concept, see George R. Husband, "The Entity Concept in Accounting," *Accounting Review* (October 1954), pp. 552-63; Robert T. Sprouse, "The Significance of the Concept of the Corporation in Accounting Analysis," *Accounting Review* (July 1957), pp. 369-78; W.A. Paton and A.C. Littleton, *An Introduction to Corporate Accounting Standards* (American Accounting Association, 1940), pp. 43 ff.

5. In 1972 the composite dividend yield of stocks in the Standard and Poor's Index was 2.70 percent.

6. Eric L. Kohler, *A Dictionary for Accountants*, 4th ed. (Englewood Cliffs, N.J.: Prentice-Hall, 1970).

7. Accounting Principles Board, *Statement No. 4*, par. 90.

8. 3 Wis: R.R.C.D. 623, 631 (1905).

9. W.P. Hilton, "Interest on Capital," *Journal of Accountancy* (October 1916).

10. Reported by C.H. Scovell in "Interest on Investment," *American Economic Review* (March 1919).

11. Reported in C.H. Scovell, *Interest as a Cost* (New York: Ronald Press, 1924).

12. William Morse Cole, "Interest on Investment in Equipment," *Journal of Accountancy* (April 1913).

13. American Institute of Accountants, *1918 Yearbook*, "Report of the Special Committee on Interest in Relation to Cost," pp. 110-12.

14. *Accounting Theory* by William A. Paton, 1922. Reprinted 1962 by Accounting Studies Press, Ltd., Chicago, p. 271.

15. See especially his *Interest as a Cost*.

16. Study Group on Business Income, *Changing Concepts of Business Income* (New York: Macmillan Company, 1952).

17. Charles F. Schlatter and William J. Schlatter, *Cost Accounting*, 2nd ed. (New York: Wiley, 1939).

18. The following books do not even discuss the possibility of recording equity interest: John W. Coughlan, *Guide to Contemporary Theory of Accounts* (Englewood Cliffs, N.J.: Prentice-Hall, 1965); Eldon S. Hendreksen, *Accounting Theory*, rev. ed. (Homewood, Ill.: Richard D. Irwin, 1970); Roland Frank Salmonson, *Basic Financial Accounting Theory* (Belmont, Calif.: Wadsworth Publishing Co., 1969). S. A. Zeff and Thomas F. Keller, *Financial Accounting Theory* (New York: McGraw-Hill, 1965), a book of readings, has no reading on this topic nor, so far as I can determine, is the topic even mentioned. Paul Grady's *Inventory of Generally Accepted Accounting Principles for Business Enterprises*, Accounting Research Study No. 7 (New York: American Institute of Certified Public Accountants, 1965) does not mention the subject. Also, Paul H. Jeynes deals with a related topic in *Profitability and Economic Choice* (Iowa State University Press, 1968).

19. Harold Bierman, Jr. *Financial Accounting Theory* (New York: Macmillan Company, 1965), pp. 58, 59.

20. Glenn A. Welsch, Charles Zlatkovich, and John A. White, *Intermediate Accounting*, 3rd ed. (Homewood, Ill.; Richard D. Irwin, 1972) p. 484.

21. Robert T. Sprouse and Maurice Moonitz, *A Tentative Set of Broad Accounting Principles for Business Enterprises* (New York: American Institute of Certified Public Accountants, 1962), p. 55.

22. "Fixed Asset Accounting: The Capitalization of Cost," *Management Accounting* (January 1973).

23. For example, Mey and Most included interest as one of the elements of cost in their proposed system of replacement value accounting. Abram Mey and Kenneth S. Most, "Replacement Value Accounting," *The Accountant* (September 7, 1963) pp. 275-80.

24. G.J. Pierce, *The Measurement of Capital Employed* (London: Business Books Ltd., 1970).

25. Glenn A. Welsch and Lewis F. Davidson, "Issues in Accounting for Interest Costs," Working Paper 73-15 (Austin: University of Texas, Graduate School of Business, 1973).

26. Philip L. Defliese, *Should Accountants Capitalize Leases?* (New York: Cooper and Lybrand, 1973).

27. Federal Power Commission, *Uniform System of Accounts Prescribed for Public Utilities and Licensees* (Washington: U.S. Government Printing Office, 1937) p. 42.

28. James C. Bonbright, *Principles of Public Utility Rates* (New York: Columbia University Press, 1961) p. 180.

29. American Institute of CPAs, 1972, pp. 191, 192.

30. See *SEC Release No. 33-5505*, which proposes a moratorium on such practices as of June 21, 1974.

31. Welsch and Davidson, "Issues in Accounting for Interest Costs," p. 37.

32. Albert Bradley, "Financial Control Policies of General Motors Corporation and Their Relationship to Cost Accounting," *N.A.C.A. Bulletin* (January 1, 1927).

33. U.S. Atomic Energy Commission, *Annual Report*, 1973,

34. American Institute of Real Estate Appraisers, *The Appraisal of Real Estate*, 5th ed., p. 268.

Chapter 3
Implications for Financial Reporting

1. From "Theodore Limperg and His Theory of Values and Costs" by Abram Mey, *Abacus* (Sidney University Press, September 1966), p. 5.

2. Philip L. Defliese, *Should Accountants Capitalize Leases?* (New York: Coopers & Lybrand, 1973).

3. Adapted from ibid, p. 18.

4. Accounting Principles Board, *Basic Concepts and Accounting Prin-*

ciples Underlying Financial Statements of Business Enterprises (October 1970).

5. Glenn A. Welsch and Lewis F. Davidson, *Issues in Accounting for Interest Costs*, Working Paper 73-15, (Austin: University of Texas, Graduate School of Business, 1973) pp. 18-25.

Chapter 4
Implications for Public Policy

1. *Congressional Record*, May 16, 1973, p. *S*9260. This sample is not, of course, a representative cross section of defense contractors, and methodological questions can be raised about the analysis. See also Arthur E. Burns, "Profit Limitation: Regulated Industries and the Defense-Space Industries," *Bell Journal of Economics and Management Science* (1972), pp. 3-24.

2. Among the studies are one by the Logistics Management Institute in 1967 and those made for the Industry Advisory Council of the Department of Defense in 1965, 1968, 1969, 1970, and 1971.

3. This is also recommended by Arthur Andersen & Co. See its statement to the Cost Accounting Standards Board, *Cost Accounting Standards for Defense Contracts* (1972), p. 58.

4. Wilfrid Schreiber, "The Social Function of Profits," *Management International*, (1969/2-3) pp. 69-76.

5. Douglas G. Cordeman, "ASPR: Some Suggested Changes," *Management Accounting* (February 1973), p. 42.

6. *Congressional Globe* (predecessor to the Congressional Record), 37th Cong., 2d sess., quoted in *Seidman's Legislative History*, Tax Act of 1862, p. 1039.

7. For a discussion of this point, see Edward Barrett and Gerald Holtz, "The Case Against One Set of Books," *Financial Executive* (September 1972).

Chapter 5
Implications for Management Accounting

1. In his "Return on Investment: The Relation of Book-Yield to True-Yield," in *Research in Accounting Measurement* (Chicago: American Accounting Association, 1966), Ezra Solomon explores this point in depth.

2. This point was called to my attention by Chei-Min Paik and is developed more fully in his unpublished paper "A Case of the Conflict

Between Influence Systems: EOQ *vs*. ROI." (George Washington University, 1974).

3. For an elaboration of this point, see John Dearden, "The Case Against ROI Control," *Harvard Business Review* (May-June 1969), pp. 124 ff.; and David Solomons, *Divisional Peformance Measurement and Control* (Financial Executives Institute, 1965).

4. For a description of the General Electric System, see Robert N. Anthony, John Dearden, and Richard F. Vancil, *Management Control Systems*, rev. ed. (Homewood, III.: Richard D. Irwin, 1972), p. 137. For a summary of the practices of 2658 companies, see John J. Mauriel and Robert N. Anthony, "Misevaluation of Investment Center Performance," *Harvard Business Review* (March-April 1966).

5. A somewhat different approach to divisional performance measurement is described in Keith Schwayder in "A Proposed Modification to Residual Income—Interest Adjusted Income," *The Accounting Review* (April 1970), pp. 299-307.

Chapter 6
Measuring Interest Cost

1. See APB *Opinion No. 21* on amortization of premium and discount and *APB Opinion No. 26* on early extinguishment of debt issue.

2. See, for example, Eugene F. Brigham, ed., *Readings in Managerial Finance* (New York: Holt, Rinehart and Winston, 1971). This widely used book contains five articles in the section "Valuation and Financial Structure: Cost of Capital," and has references to many others. None of the five articles suggests an objective way of finding g. I have had an interesting correspondence with Paul H. Jeynes, one of the few people who claim to be able to make an objective calculation. His approach is described in Reuben E. Slesinger and Paul H. Jeynes, "Profit Incentive: Earnings Less Cost of Capital," *Accounting and Business Research*, number 7 (Summer 1972), p. 163; and "The Common Shareholder's Profit." *Consulting Engineer* 33 no. 5 (November 1972): 116.

3. The foregoing is a highly simplified version of the approach to calculating the cost of capital. For a more complete description, see Pearson Hunt, Charles M. Williams, and Gordon Donaldson, *Basic Business Finance* (4th ed.; Homewood, Ill.: Richard D. Irwin, 1970).

4. William Beaver, Paul Kettler, and Myron Scholes "The Association Between Market Determined and Accounting Determined Risk Measures," *Accounting Review* (October 1970), pp. 654-82; and R. Hamada "Portfolio Analysis, Market Equilibrium, and Corporation Finance," *Journal of Finance* (March 1969).

5. Joel Stern, (vice president, Chase Manhattan Bank NA) "Free Cash Flow—The Real Indicator of Market Performance" (July 16, 1973), unpublished memorandum.

6. Thomas R. Stauffer, "The Measurement of Corporate Rates of Return: A Generalized Formulation," *Bell Journal of Economics and Management Science* (Autumn 1971), pp. 434-69.

7. Philip L. Defliese, *Should Accountants Capitalize Leases?* (New York: Coopers & Lybrand, 1973), p. 18.

8. Arthur Andersen & Co., *Cost Accounting Standards for Defense Contracts* (Chicago 1972), p. 53.

9. See, for example, Otto Eckstein, *Water Resources Development: The Economics of Project Evaluation* (Cambridge, Mass.: Harvard University Press, 1961): Jacob A. Stockfish, "The Interest Rate Applicable to Government Investment Projects," in Hinrichs and Taylor, *Program-Budgeting and Benefit-Cost Analysis* (Pacific Palisades, Calif.: Goodyear, 1969); William J. Baumol, "On the Appropriate Discount Rate for Evaluation of Public Projects," (also in Hinrichs and Taylor); George J. Stigler, *Capital and Rates of Return in Manufacturing Industries* (Princeton, N.J.: Princeton University Press, 1963).

10. Personal communication to the author.

11. See J.D. Coughlan and W.K. Strand, *Depreciation: Accounting, Taxes, and Business Decisions* (New York: Ronald Press, 1969), ch. 2.

Chapter 7
Accounting Procedures

1. Philip L. Defliese, *Should Accountants Capitalize Leases?* (New York: Coopers & Lybrand , 1973).

2. Silvern proposes that interest on equity capital be shown as a separate asset item on the balance sheet. To me, showing this component of cost separately is unnecessary and implies a greater distinction between this and other elements of cost than is warranted. See David Harold Silvern, "Enterprise Income: Measuring Financial Management," *Financial Executive* (April 1975), p. 56.

Chapter 8
Implementation

1. See J.D. Coughlan and W.K. Strand, *Depreciation Accounting, Taxes, and Business Decisions* (New York: Ronald Press, 1969), ch. 2.

2. *Report of the Study Group on Objectives of Financial Statements* (New York: AICPA, 1973).

Index

Index

About the Author

Robert N. Anthony has broad experience in business, in government, and in academia. He has consulted for companies ranging in size from a small retail store to Exxon and General Motors. Currently he is a director of two "Fortune 500" companies.

He has worked for various government agencies over a period of thirty-five years. In 1965-68 he was Assistant Secretary of Defense, Comptroller. He is a consultant to the Federal Trade Commission and to the Cost Accounting Standards Board.

He is the author or coauthor of some fourteen books. His *Management Accounting*, now in its fifth edition, was the first modern text on this subject. He has been on the faculty of Harvard Business School since 1940, and since 1965 has been Ross Graham Walker Professor of Management Control. In 1973-74, he was President of the American Accounting Association.

Related Lexington Books

Cash Management: An Inventory Control Approach by Richard B. Homonoff and David W. Mullins, Jr. 128 pp., 1975.

Corporate Bankruptcy in America by Edward I. Altman, 208 pp., 1971

Capital Market Equilibrium and Efficiency: Implications for Accounting, Financial, and Portfolio Decision Making by James L. Bicksler. In Press.

Interest Rates on Savings Deposits: Theory, Estimation and Policy by Myron B. Slovin and Marie E. Sushka. 176 pp., 1975.

Portfolio Aspects of Corporate Capital Budgeting: Methods of Analysis, Survey of Applications and a Model by E. Eugene Carter, 256 pp., 1974.

Risk and Uncertainty in Accounting and Finance edited by John P. Dickinson, 1975.